Travels with Bertha

First published in 2012 by
Liberties Press
7 Rathfarnham Road | Terenure | Dublin 6W
Tel: +353 (1) 405 5701
www.libertiespress.com | info@libertiespress.com

Trade enquiries to Gill & Macmillan Distribution
Hume Avenue | Park West | Dublin 12
T: +353 (1) 500 9534 | F: +353 (1) 500 9595 | E: sales@gillmacmillan.ie

Distributed in the UK by
Turnaround Publisher Services
Unit 3 | Olympia Trading Estate | Coburg Road | London N22 6TZ
T: +44 (0) 20 8829 3000 | E: orders@turnaround-uk.com

Distributed in the United States by
Dufour Editions | PO Box 7 | Chester Springs | Pennsylvania 19425

Copyright © Paul Martin, 2012
The author has asserted his moral rights.

ISBN: 978-1-907593-42-0
2 4 6 8 10 9 7 5 3 1
A CIP record for this title is available from the British Library.

Cover design by Sin É Design
Internal design by Liberties Press

Travels with Bertha

Two years exploring Australia in a 1978 Ford Stationwagon

Paul Martin

LIB
ERT
IES

To Len and Rob – for friendship

and

To Samuele, Luca and Damiano
– don't always listen when people tell you things can't be done

Unless, of course, it's your father talking

Contents

Sydney: Year Two

Across the Continent to Perth

Western Australia

The Top End: Closing The Circle

Acknowledgements

The original draft of this book was written in California over a three year period shortly after leaving Australia. My thanks go to those few friends, including Rory Hogan, who persevered through that early version.

Realising how the experiences of young people travelling down to Australia during another recession so strongly paralleled mine in the mid to late 1990s, *Travels with Bertha* was updated with more historical background and fully revised for publication in 2010 and 2011.

I particularly want to express my appreciation to Gerry Mullins for his advice and encouragement while completing this book. My thanks also go to Catherine O'Brien for producing the many travel maps and to everyone who read later drafts and gave their valuable feedback, including all at Liberties Press. Any errors and imperfections that remain, it hardly needs to be said, are fully mine.

Although I refer to various historical writings, I particularly drew on Robert Hughes's *The Fatal Shore*, an essential read for those interested in the early colonial period.

Finally, thanks to Barbara, for her long hours of babysitting in Svarchi while I completed the book – and for all those many other things besides.

Voyage within you, on the fabled ocean,
And you will find the Southern Continent

from *Terra Australis* by James McAuley

I would live all my life in nonchalance and insouciance
Were it not for making a living which is rather a nouciance

Ogden Nash

Sydney: Year One

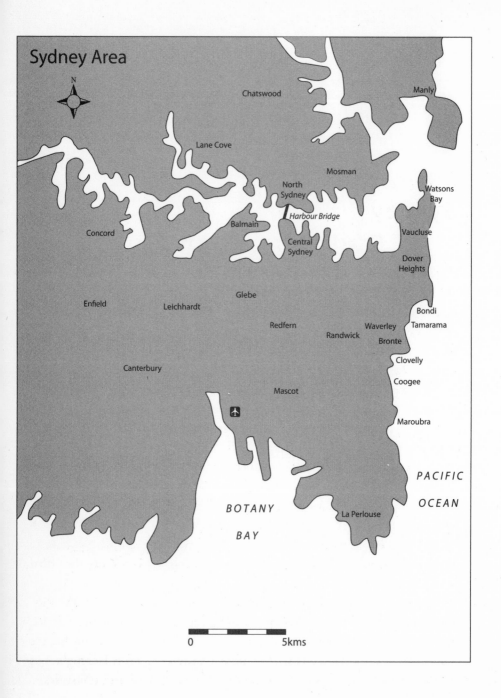

Sydney

Arriving into Sydney, my blood turned cold. Out of the corner of my eye I spotted a police bloodhound bounding down the airport concourse and suddenly stop at my backpack. Clouded by jet-lag and nerves, I just *knew* he'd sniff out my box of muesli and I'd be deported for smuggling before I'd properly set foot in the country. But he soon just waddled off like the carefree puppy he seemed to be. When I declared my suspect package to the customs official moments later, he seemed just as unfazed. 'I reckon we might just be able to let that one go, mate.' And with a laconic smile, I was waved into Australia.

But on the shuttle bus into town, my anxiety returned. This was late June, midwinter in Australia – something I'd neglected to bear in mind during my exhaustive travel preparations – and peering out the rain-speckled window all I could see was a grey, wet city. A glimpse of the harbour bridge appeared through a gap in two far-off buildings, so I knew this had to be Sydney. But what about the sunshine, surfie beaches and easy living I'd heard so much about? By the time we pulled up outside a rundown hostel in King's Cross, in what was obviously a red-light district, I was getting very concerned. Just what was going on?

King's Cross lies about two kilometres from the centre of the city. Cut through Hyde Park, travel up the rising expanse of King William Street, turn left at the enormous flashing neon Coca-Cola sign, and you hit the strip clubs, fast food restaurants, backpacker hostels and many late-night bars of 'the Cross'. King's Cross is frequented by sailors, drug addicts, transvestites, strippers, hookers and crime gangs – but, undeterred, thousands of backpackers seem to check into its many hostels each year. Because, despite appearances, it is a very safe and authentic introduction to backpacker Australia.

Throwing my backpack on the one undishevelled bed in the shabby hostel dorm, I quickly went out to meander around King's Cross's chilly streets for several hours, before returning to the hostel to sleep off my jet-lag. Waking up in the early evening, I heard someone moving around the room. Glancing up from my jacket, which was doubling up as my bedcover – I'd yet to buy a sleeping bag and the hostel management obviously saw no need for blankets – I saw a blue face peering up at me sorrowfully from beneath a 1990s' Take That haircut. Then unbidden, in thick Yorkshire, it spoke.

'I am right, aren't I?' the voice asked mournfully. 'This is Australia? Well I thought this place were meant to be warm. Cos back 'ome I watch *'Ome and Away* and you never see any of them bastards wearing a sweater, now do ya? Well sod them, I'm freezing!'

And so I met Rob.

Rob seemed to be having a hard time with the weather. He'd been on holidays in Australia three years before and had encountered a much different climate. He'd flown in at noon, made his way straight down to Bondi beach, enjoyed unprotected sunshine for several hours, and then spent the next three days in bed with second-degree sunstroke.

Consequently, this time he'd decided to travel light and now hadn't a single sweater or jacket among the mound of T-shirts and jeans falling out of his backpack. But it was a cold winter night, our hostel room was *very* well ventilated, and he was frozen, miserable and jet-lagged. I gave him a present of my spare sweater. Slightly warmer, he grinned at me: 'Fancy a beer?'

Within the hour, Rob had introduced me to Anthony, a friend from home who'd already been in the country six months. As an old hand, Anthony immediately took command and determined that a pub-crawl was in order. So we caught a train to Circular Quay and walked along the harbour-side up to the Rocks, the old settlement of Sydney.

Rejuvenated from its badly rundown state in the 1960s and 70s, the Rocks, with its 'old worldie' feel, has now become a prime tourist destination. And its charm is real. Walking through it in the darkness, I gazed up at the names lit up above the pub doors – the Lord Nelson, the Duke of Wellington, the

Mercantile, the Hero of Waterloo – and felt that time had stood still since the days of the First Fleet and the Battle of Trafalgar.

'That's what ya drink in New South Wales,' Anthony said, slapping a three-quarter-pint glass of beer in front of me in the Lord Nelson. 'A schooner!' And so began the evening – and my two-and-a-half-year stay in Australia.

For the next few hours, Rob and Anthony kept me entertained as they tried to outdo each other with stories about their travels and with gossip about people back home in Leeds. I was all the more amused as Rob had a lisp and Anthony had a stutter. Although they'd known each other for years, both seemed surprised when I mentioned it.

'I always knew you t-t-talked funny, Bobble! See, you've a bloody lisp. You c-c-can get help for t-t-that, you know!'

'It's-s not me who talks-s funny, you daft bas-stard. Didn't you hear him? You're the one with the bloody s-stutter.'

After a few drinks in the Hero of Waterloo, we tumbled out the door in convulsions, only to abruptly fall silent as the spectacle of the underside of the Harbour Bridge appeared, towering massively above us. Craning our necks, we looked up at the enormous metal girders as our breath turned frosty in the night air. Hushed but exhilarated, we made our way quickly to the next pub.

Seeing the Mercantile's two pool tables, Anthony quickly devised a plan. He'd challenge an innocent to a game. He'd lose a small bet on the first game, lose more on a second, and finally, with a greatly increased stake, nail his opponent on the third. I later saw Anthony play sober and he really was an excellent pool player. Unfortunately, by now he'd drunk so much that he had difficulty staying on his feet, let alone wield a pool cue in a masterly fashion. So I wasn't surprised when everything went perfectly according to plan until the final game. By then he'd lost eighty dollars. Sending Rob rummaging through his pockets, he slammed the peculiar sum of one hundred and twenty-three dollars on the side. As he staggered past me to the table to break, he stuttered softly in my ear: 'Paul, just like t-t-taking c-c-candy from a baby.'

Unfortunately, the baby took the candy from him. But somehow it all seemed wonderfully funny, and crying out 'Sure it's only money!' – as if two hundred dollars were only loose change and we wouldn't soon be eking out the church-mouse existence of a backpacker – we tottered off to the next pub, the Jackson on George.

The evening became a blur from then on. Rob quickly fell asleep on a bar stool and Anthony's stutter soon became indecipherable. Joining a group of Irish nurses, I listened as one of them lamented about the white marks on the bare ring fingers of the three middle-aged men trying to chat them up. But I wasn't really paying attention. Australian accents broke through the hubbub of the bar, and my mind wandered. Unfamiliar colours and logos – for Victoria Bitter, Tooheys Blue, Cascade beer and the Polar Bear logo of Bundaberg Rum – lit up the pub all around me. Cocooned in a drunken haze, I considered the twenty thousand kilometres I'd just come. I'd travelled the length of the globe and short of flying to the moon, I'd never be able to travel so far again. My sense of the world suddenly changed and I felt the freefall of vast distances yawn open inside of me. It was then that I finally realised that Ireland was now a world away. That was the moment I really arrived in Australia.

Settling In

I spent my first few weeks in Sydney with Rob and Anthony enjoying the nightlife. We drank, went to clubs, toured the city and began to get a taste for Australia.

One night in the Soho bar in King's Cross, we saw two men who'd been chatting together amiably only minutes earlier stand up from their table, walk calmly outside and begin pummelling each other up and down the street. Rushing out, the horrified bar manageress screamed frantically at the circle of male spectators to break it up. But the crowd just continued to gaze on in admiration at the two men's fighting skills and seemed genuinely appalled at her lack of etiquette.

'Ah *lady*! Fair fight!' they lamented to the spoilsport. 'One on one, lady! Fair go!' The melee swung up and down the street, before disappearing out of sight. The winner, his hair tousled and his T-shirt ripped, returned shortly afterwards snorting blood and condensation out into the night air. What became of the loser I didn't see. Australia, it seemed, was still a man's world.

But the fun and exorbitant spending soon ended when Rob and Anthony both left the city. Anthony's one sibling had moved down to Australia seven years before, and his parents were unwilling to lose another son to such a distant continent. So, paying her airfare, they despatched his girlfriend from England to bring him back alive. It was difficult not to notice either her dress-sense or her physical appearance, both of which were strikingly like Pamela

Anderson's. So it was hard to fault Anthony when he left for England with her a week later.

Rob wasn't long in leaving either. Picking up a relocation van – which was supplied free by the rental company provided it was driven back to the point where it was originally hired – he drove across the continent to Perth, where he was to remain for the next five months. Later, he admitted that flying might have been a better idea: the cost of fuelling such a heavy van four thousand kilometres across the continent had come to more than the price of the air ticket, and besides, the drive had nearly killed him.

The fatigue would tell in his voice as he rang me most evenings from a lonely service station to assure me he hadn't met with an accident and turned into dingo fodder. After driving for ten hours, he'd tell me in a leaden voice about roaming emus, hovering eagles and the countless other wonders he'd seen on that day's drive through hundreds of kilometres of outback. Listening to him down the receiver in my distant Sydney flat, he set my imagination free. When would I ever get to see these outback places for myself?

A few weeks before, just after my arrival, the reality of my living circumstances and my hefty bank loan had focused my mind on the need to find work.

Hostel living, I was finding, was a great way to meet people and gain local knowledge about accommodation and work; my main problem was simply staying sober. Besides needing sleep and a reasonably clear head to do the rounds of the employment agencies, living in the hostel meant I had no contact number to give prospective employers. I simply had to get my own place.

And so, a little groggy, I set to it on my third morning in Australia. A backpacker had told me that I'd find a flat in the classified section of Saturday's *Sydney Morning Herald*. But as I read through the ads, none of the place names meant anything to me: Surry Hills, Glebe, Darling Point, Potts Point, Coogee, North Ryde, Newtown, Bondi . . . Bondi! Now, I'd heard of that. Looking at the map, I saw Waverley and Bronte were nearby and, attracted on a whim by their pleasant literary associations, I set off.

Taking the short train ride from King's Cross to Bondi Junction, I was soon walking up to the quaint neighbourhood of Waverley. The second address circled by red biro in my newspaper was on Wiley Street, a delightful, sleepy street of broad, shady trees and chirping birds. Ringing the bell of a charming wooden house, I was met by a good-looking girl who introduced herself as Dominique. She invited me in and offered me a shortbread biscuit and tea in a china cup and saucer.

Dominique was an English and history teacher in what I later discovered was a very exclusive Anglican boys' boarding school. She enjoyed sharing with travellers, she said. They were usually interesting and always had good stories to tell. Her current roommate was just moving back to her native Tokyo. I was shown her room, which was glowing with afternoon sunshine and was bare except for the honeyed floorboards, a single neat mattress and a bamboo clothes rack.

I was so delightfully impressed by the house, and Dominique's almost colonial sense of decorum and refinement, that I replied to all her questions in the appropriate manner. I'd studied literature in college, I told her. I'd lived in Italy for a year, I said. And the following Monday I'd be starting work with a fund management company in Martin Place.

As I'd been in the country less than three days, the last statement wasn't altogether true. But she liked stories, and I wanted to move in, so where, I reckoned, was the harm? The following Saturday, I arrived with my backpack and moved into the first of the four flats I would share in Sydney over the next two years.

Visiting the temp agencies the following week didn't prove to be as tedious as I'd expected. Sweltering in a shirt and tie, I'd sit in line with dozens of other hopefuls, reading out-of-date magazines, waiting to hand in carefully doctored CVs and undergo an apparently endless series of data-entry and typing tests. The test results always made me feel remarkably unemployable, but then I hadn't counted on the peculiar interviews that generally followed.

Most of the temp consultants, being Australians in their twenties, had feet every bit as itchy as ours, and they certainly weren't going to waste the opportunity to pick the brains of this daily flood of European backpackers flowing through their doors. So, much to my relief, instead of being quizzed about my work skills and my chequered employment history, I was asked about Europe. Specific questions related to Swedish women, Guinness, the Pamploma bull festival and the Oktoberfest. Quickly exhausting my limited experience of the Oktoberfest (I had none of Pamploma or of Swedish women, alas), I'd switch to the subjects of cheap Spanish wine and warm English beer before finishing off on the mystical properties of authentic Guinness – all recounted in a strong Irish accent. This had the desired effect, and a week later I was given an assignment in a large international bank in the city centre.

My one-year Australian visa stipulated that I could only work three months at any one job, but in 1995 no one seemed to bother with such legal technicalities. Still, I would have been surprised, on entering the intimidating grandeur of the bank's skyscraper lobby that Monday morning, to know that I wouldn't be leaving there for another fourteen months.

But rather than being a place of ambitious careerists, the bank had a very relaxed and fun-loving atmosphere, and I soon settled in nicely. And it didn't much help this leisurely work ethic that in my first few months the place was overrun with temps (mostly backpackers) who'd been brought in to deal with the bank's administrative backlogs. Although perhaps not the greatest of HR policies, it certainly did wonders for the social life of the place. Not a Friday went by without a very liquid lunchtime send-off for yet another temp leaving to travel up the Queensland coast. Friday afternoons, it hardly needs to be said – even by exacting Australian standards – tended not to be the most productive.

But despite my leisurely work environment, I was still trying to find my way around in this new country. My new home in Waverley was only minutes from the Eastern Beaches of Bondi, Tamarama, Bronte, Clovelly, Coogee and Maroubra, all of which lie to the south of the harbour mouth (but to the east of the city) and straddle the high coastline like rosary beads.

The first time I saw the beaches was with Rob a week after I'd moved in. It was a dull midwinter Sunday afternoon, and he'd called up, after two weeks in the Spartan surroundings of the hostel, to experience the creature comforts of home once more. After a cup of tea and some television, we went out for a walk. Not knowing where we were going, we just ambled along aimlessly for the next half-hour while he entertained me with stories about back home in Yorkshire. But turning a corner, he stopped in mid-sentence as Tamarama beach and the ocean opened up hazily in front of us.

I'd always imagined that seeing the expanse of the Pacific for the first time would be an overpowering experience, but the day was too dull, and it just looked like Dublin bay. Besides, Rob always kept me down to earth. Having left school at sixteen, he always gave me a hard time if I used 'one of 'em big fancy words!' There was no pretence about Rob. He'd a big heart, a great sense of humour and a clear Yorkshire view of the world – and I suppose that's why I came to like him so much.

We walked down to the beach and, instead of marvelling at the wonders of nature, we just hopped along the surf like schoolboys or clambered among the weirdly shaped sand-walls. A grey sky lay low over the sea and, although neither of us mentioned it, the indistinct mass of the murky sea seemed to stretch on forever, and home really did feel like a world away.

After Rob left for Perth, I'd occasionally walk the high coast-line path along the Eastern Beaches on weekends. And passing through Clovelly graveyard, lying along the path high above the ocean, I remember first sensing Australia's eerie sense of impassivity and remoteness.

Rows of headstones stand forgotten in the sunshine. And even though thousands of people must walk through it each year, the graveyard still has a wild air about it. As I knew few people in my first few months, I'd occasionally spent an hour there at a time deciphering the headstones.

Although there are several Italians, most of the gravestones belong to the nationalities which came to Australia before the Second World War: English, Scottish, Irish, Germans, even a few Americans. In particular, there are many from the late colonial period and the first few decades after Federation in 1901. Carved onto the stone are the names of sons lost in battle or at sea; beloved daughters taken by fever; mothers and wives lost in childbirth; or fathers, who for decades worked at their trades. One headstone reads to 'Horace ... [his surname has been eroded away by the salty sea air] aged 7, drowned at sea in 1911'. By his side are the graves of his parents, who died over twenty and forty years later. Alongside the date of death, the place of birth was given on all the headstones; it always seemed to be somewhere very far away.

Reading those headstones, I realised how fortunate I was. For the price of a few weeks' pay, I could always catch a flight and be back in Ireland in a few days. For people coming to Australia as recently as half a century previously, there was no such luxury.

First Impressions

Water, or perhaps more accurately the ocean, is the overwhelming presence for the first-time visitor to Sydney. Dominated as it is by the vast harbour, Sydney has a seemingly endless expanse of coastline – which makes Cook's decision in 1770 to land in Botany Bay and not within the confines of the harbour all the more peculiar.

As a consequence, the reality of Botany Bay (which like many I had mistakenly believed to lie within the harbour) came as a shock to the eleven wooden ships of the First Fleet at the end of their extraordinary voyage in 1788. After crossing three oceans, they must have considered themselves fortunate that in an era of primitive sea travel, of crammed and unsanitary conditions below deck, of rampant typhus, scurvy and brutality on board, that they had lost only forty-eight of the almost thousand people on board.

In some respects, it was only after the First Fleet had anchored that their real hardships began. By the time the ships set sail, Captain Cook had been dead for over eight years – he'd been stabbed, beaten and then hacked to death by natives in Hawaii in 1779. So when the fleet and the new colony were being planned, the authorities turned for instruction to Henry Banks, Cook's chief botanist on his voyage of 1770.

The choice of Australia for Britain's new penal colony had come indirectly out of the defeat in the American War of Independence in 1778. With the loss of the American colonies and the convict dumping grounds in Virginia and Maryland, alternative locations, such as the west coast of Africa, Canada and even Gibraltar, were considered, and soon discounted. Finally, the Home Office opted for Botany Bay in New South Wales, which Cook had discovered on his first *Endeavour* voyage almost two decades before.

There were compelling reasons for the founding of this new penal colony in Eastern Australia. Not only were the thousands of prisoners being held in hulks in many of the river estuaries around Britain and Ireland prone to rioting, coming onto shore and spreading disease among the general populace, but commercial interests also favoured it. The Dutch (who had already claimed Australia's west coast the century before), but primarily the French, had been prowling around the Crown colony of Eastern Australia, and Britain feared for its commercial and imperial interests in the Indian and Pacific Oceans. If a permanent colony was established on the southern continent, it would secure Britain's claims to the region's nautical routes, in particular those to the Indies, the Orient and southern Africa.

Indeed, when the First Fleet eventually landed in Sydney, these fears were shown to be well founded, as they encountered the French navigator, La Perouse, who had arrived only days before. He dined with the officers, acknowledged their prior territorial claim, and had the graciousness to remark that '*Enfin Monsieur Cook a tant fait, qu'il ne m'a rien laissé à faire, que d'admirer ses oeuvres.*' ('Truly Monsieur Cook accomplished so much that there's nothing left for me to do but admire his achievements'). He then set sail out into the Pacific, was swallowed up by the ocean and was never seen again. A suburb at the far end of the Eastern Beaches now bears his name.

But when the Home Office turned to Banks in the 1780s for more information about Botany Bay, the intervening years seemed to have played strange tricks with his memory. It's true that Cook had committed an unaccountable and uncharacteristic error in reporting that the land around Botany Bay was rich and fertile, but it was Banks' additions which were most responsible for falsifying the expectations of the budding colonists.

When the fleet set sail from England, it expected finally to come to anchor in a place with rich topsoil and only a thin tree cover, which would make clearing unnecessary and allow farming to thrive. There would be plenty of stone for building, and the anchorage was reported to be deep and well protected from the violence of the ocean. But instead, Philip's fleet sailed into a shallow, exposed bay bordered by a flat, infertile plain of dry scrub and eucalyptus trees.

They discovered at first hand that Cook had named the place out of regard for the forays of Banks and his fellow botanist, and not on account of any lush vegetation. This was certainly not a spot where a new settlement could survive.

So within days, Phillip, the colony's first governor, set sail to Port Jackson, twenty kilometres up the coast – a place which Cook had observed, though not entered, eighteen years before. The fleet sailed through the harbour promontories and dropped anchor, and the first white Australian settlement – a penal colony – was founded in the southern continent on 27 January 1778.

As Robert Hughes recounts in *The Fatal Shore*, Philip was exultant at this new harbour. In a letter to Lord Sydney, the Admiralty Secretary after whom he quickly renamed the natural wonder, he described the inlet as 'the finest harbour in the world, in which a thousand sail of the line may ride with the most perfect security'.

The disembarkation of the women didn't take place until 6 February. After the sailors were issued rum freely, they joined with the male convicts in chasing the women and then raping or copulating with them along the rocks of the harbour near where the present-day Botanic Gardens lie.

The ships' officers were horrified by the orgy. But they soon found that they had a more pressing matter to deal with – the very survival of the colony. With few trained farmers or tradesmen, and little in the way of foodstuffs or irrigation, most of the crops failed in the next few years, and starvation seemed a very likely prospect. Only by the strictest rationing and severest of floggings for stealing did the colony hold out until the arrival of the Second Fleet two and a half years later, in June 1790. Australia, it was clear from the start, was no place for the faint-hearted.

It's little surprise, therefore, that for at least the first half-century of the colony, most visitors of rank viewed Australia as a hellhole they had to share with native savages and the bestial dregs of their now-abandoned civilisation. And unlike the Aborigines, who found an abundance of foodstuffs in roots and vegetation, in hunting and fishing, early colonial commentators found few natural resources or physical beauty in this continent of glaring, unendingly dry landscapes. The place seemed so barbaric and inhospitable that it could rot a man alive.

Robert Ross, the first lieutenant governor, wrote that: 'in the whole world there is not a worse country'. David Collins, another ship's officer, wrote to his family that 'I am spending the Prime of my Life at the farthest part of the World, without Credit, without Profit, secluded from my Family . . . my Connections, from the World, under constant Apprehensions of being starved. All these considerations induce me . . . to embrace the first Opportunity that offers of escaping from a country that is nothing better than a Place of banishment for the Outcasts of society.'

That sense of revulsion continued until at least the 1830s. As Australia's leading historian, Manning Clark, records: 'In 1817 John Oxley [the explorer] told the Governor of New South Wales that most of the interior . . . was uninhabitable and useless for the purposes of civilised man. . . . Charles Darwin was so appalled in January 1836 by the "useless sterility" of the country [and] the "extreme uniformity in the character of the vegetation" . . . that when he left our country he wrote in his diary that he did so "without any sorrow or regret".'

And those were the feelings of the respectable free colonists whose written expressions remain. What the mostly illiterate convicts thought, after surviving the squalor of transportation only to be washed up on this land of searing heat and hard labour, one can only imagine.

God's Country

Shortly after arriving in Sydney, I decided one sunny afternoon to go down and see the Opera House.

From its wide steps, I looked out over the full stretch of Sydney harbour, and I was mesmerised. And it wasn't the iconic shell roofs of the Opera House that left me open-mouthed; it was the walls. Why does no one ever mention that they're covered with countless thousands of square white tiles, just like bathroom ceramics? And the Harbour Bridge is so near, just a few hundred metres across the glittering water, that its massive girders seemed to be almost within touching distance. How unassumingly proud, I thought, to have these two majestic creations, the bridge and the Opera House, both within spitting distance of each other, almost as if each were good-naturedly bemused at the fuss people seemed to make of the other. Despite the jokes about Australian 'culture', *that*, I thought, showed grandeur!

In the square below me, a bagpiper in full traditional costume was playing plaintive highland tunes which drifted up to the Opera House and out over the water. A sign at his laced-up feet asked for donations to help send him to the World Scottish Music Championships in Edinburgh later that year. Excited Japanese tourists came up to put their arm around him and snap a photo. They would bow courteously and smile amiably but, despite all their fine manners, they never put so much as a cent into his instrument case. I smiled wryly at the scene, but the sound of the bagpipes gave me a twinge of longing, evoking somewhere that, I felt instinctively, I wouldn't be seeing for a long time.

For a few minutes, as my eyes took all this in, it seemed that the person sitting here on the hard concrete steps of the Opera House, gazing out over Sydney Harbour, was someone else. How could this be me?

'The worst part of travel,' Paul Theroux once wrote, 'the most emotional, is the sight of people leading ordinary lives.' That's how I felt that afternoon. All around me in Sydney, and I knew back in Ireland, people were getting on with their daily lives: going to work, meeting up with their romantic partners, visiting their families, drinking with friends. But instead, here I was at the far end of the world living the limbo-life of a temporary resident, twenty-five, jobless, and very much alone. And despite all this, I still had only the haziest notion of why I was here.

In my time in Australia, I was to hear many interesting tales about why people had come; most seemed to involve either escape or a search for something that seemed to elude them in the confining familiarity of home.

In Queensland, an Englishman told me how, feeling devastated after his wife had left him, he had taken to drink. Sitting alone in the pub one night, he mulled over how to connect two odd-sized pipes stored in his garage and fix them to the exhaust of his car to gas himself. With the technical problem solved in his head, he made to leave. But then he met a friend whom he hadn't seen for years at the pub door. She asked what was up and he replied with black humour: 'Oh, nothing much, I'm just off home to kill myself.' When he briefly told her why, she just said: 'You do that, and who's going to take care of your baby daughter?' Hearing that, he broke down crying at the pub entrance. But for that chance encounter, he told me, he'd now be dead. He'd left for Australia soon afterwards.

A white South African I knew of had come to Australia after shooting a black intruder in post-apartheid Johannesburg. The courts acquitted him, but he had to get out. He just couldn't breathe in his home country any more. In Sydney, I knew a guy who'd escaped England because he was afraid that in another heated argument he'd snap and kill his girlfriend.

Although my story, I knew, had none of their drama, it still seemed odd to think that only two months before I'd appeared quite settled in Dublin. Like most of my friends a few years out of college, I was working in a dull, apparently dead-end job, paying just enough to cover my rent, basic bills and the price of a few weekly pints. With unemployment so high in the early 1990s, I knew the mantra of 'you're lucky to have a job' well enough. But surely, I thought, there has to be something better than this?

My enthusiasm for the job must have shown because one day, in the most thoughtful of ways, my boss invited me into her office to inform me that my temporary contract would not be renewed. Following an instant of alarm, I suddenly felt huge relief and to my boss's surprise I thanked her warmly and breezed out of the office. Within the hour, I'd made up my mind to come to Australia.

Ostensibly I was now in Australia on a 'gap year' (to apply a term only then coming into use). Presumably when my twelve-month visa expired, and with the 'bit of travelling' out of my system, I would return to Ireland, resume where I'd left off and knuckle down to a normal life. But that's not how I saw it. And I certainly had no interest in taking up where I'd left off in Dublin.

No, I had a different plan. Now it seemed to me that I could finally indulge a long-held fantasy. For years I'd wanted to escape to a faraway place, work a menial job to pay my way and, in my spare time, read just as the fancy took me.

Two books in particular had given me this idea. One was by a Welsh mariner whose boat had become ice-bound at the fall of an Arctic winter. In the months of polar darkness, he'd survived on tinned food and melted ice – and had lived in a world so strange that it had almost broken his sanity. But with springtime the light appeared, the ice cracked, and he returned home seeing the world through different eyes.

The second was Brian Keenan's *An Evil Cradling*. His mental occupations while in solitary confinement in Beirut fascinated me. All the stories he'd read, or the events he'd experienced, he'd spin through his mind like a film reel. Then he'd cut and edit each frame so intricately that it was as if he were recreating luminous worlds within the universe of his own head.

That was the sort of traveller I wanted to be: I wanted to wander freely into infinite space. What purpose lay behind this quixotic undertaking, and what would come of it, I had no idea. But if I could do it in warm sunshine, and earn as much as I was getting in Ireland, what was there to lose? Australia seemed to make perfect sense.

Or at least it had when I was planning my journey in the secure comfort of Dublin. But now, on my own and so far away, I wasn't quite so sure. Suddenly shuddering with cold, I looked up and saw the late-afternoon winter sunshine glinting off the harbour water and realised I must have been in a daydream for hours. Suddenly aware of what I'd taken on, I felt a surge of determination and knew I'd better just get on with it. So, grabbing my small backpack, I began walking briskly to Circular Quay station to catch a train back to my flat in the Eastern Suburbs.

I wasn't long in Australia before my plan got a push in the right direction. Natalie, one of my first work colleagues, had immigrated to Australia from St Petersburg in Russia only a few years before with her physicist husband and two young sons. Very affable, highly cultured and brimming with energy, she would enthuse about Australia to me. The culture was wonderful – she loved attending plays and concerts in the Opera House – and she could think of nowhere better in the world to bring up children; the country, she felt, was so healthy and free.

But it was when she told me that she still had to unpack many of her two thousand books, still boxed up in the basement of her new Sydney home, that I decided that she was the person to ask about Pushkin. Was it true, I wondered, when they say he's simply impossible to translate properly from the Russian?

Looking up from my computer screen, I saw her plump, pale face suddenly glow, as if infused by a memory. Then, drawing out the full sibilance of his name, she gasped breathlessly: 'Ahh, Puusshkin . . . !'

Inspired by this undisguised response, within days I had finished the first part of Gorky's visceral autobiography, and over the next few months I got through much of Chekhov, Pasternak, Mandelstam, Mikhail Sholokhov, and of course Tolstoy.

Being in Australia, however, I thought I really should have a go at some of its authors. 'Help yourself to anything on my shelf,' Dominque (an English teacher after all) said generously when I asked her for guidance. 'But if I were you, I'd start with Henry Lawson. That's where most people usually begin.'

Although Banjo Paterson's 'Waltzing Matilda' and 'The Man from Snowy River' are perhaps better known, arguably Lawson's works had more influence in shaping how this nation of coastal dwellers came to see itself, and came to be portrayed abroad. Lawson's stories, written for the most part in the late nine-teenth century, vividly portrayed how hard outback life had been during the colonial period. With little human company for miles around, an early Australian depended on his few neighbours to survive the physical dangers, the daily needs and the gnawing loneliness of what was then a bleak, forgotten land. Impoverished drovers and bushmen, who'd often suffered most of the worst knocks life had to offer, inevitably came to place vast importance on human camaraderie and decency, and the term 'mateship' came to describe that deep bond of loyalty between these resourceful and unpretentious people.

But Lawson, a second-generation Norwegian, wasn't blind to the downside of this narrowly focused sensibility. It may have been very suited to a hard, struggling, pioneer society (which for much of its history Australia has been), but it was not one which was always sympathetic to self-examination, or to cultural appreciation.

Lawson was therefore one of many who saw early Australia as a cultural backwater in which no artist could hope to thrive; indeed, he himself left Australia to live in England for two years at the turn of the century. In the 1890s, he acerbically advised any talented young Australian 'to go to London (or the United States or Timbuktu) rather than stay in Australia.' If such a trip were not possible, he advised 'suicide'. This sentiment was to carry credence for decades, perhaps most famously among the talented generation that left Australia in the 1950s and '60s and which included Germaine Greer, Clive James, Barry Humphries and Robert Hughes.

But mid-1990s Sydney gave no sense of being a backwater. Australians often refer to their land as 'God's country', it is so blessed with natural beauty, good living and a sense of freedom. And most backpackers coming from perennially depressed Ireland would be hard pressed to disagree. The build-up to the 2000 Olympics was beginning to be felt in construction projects, and Australia, or at least Sydney, seemed to most new arrivals to be a place of affluent and vibrant – if not utopian – living. All of which made the debate in advance of the 1996 federal election the more puzzling.

There seemed to be only two issues that year that really mattered: the economy and Paul Keating. As both Treasury Secretary (for two terms under Bob Hawke) and as Labor Prime Minister (for another two terms), Keating had been in senior political office for the last thirteen years. But Australians seemed to think that the economy was a shambles, and wanted a change. Arriving down from recessionary Ireland and walking into such well-paying temp jobs, most backpackers thought that this must be just another Australian prank. But it seemed that Australians were serious.

Keating himself was at pains to get across that the country had experienced seventeen continuous quarters of growth. But it fell on deaf ears, as John Howard, the lacklustre but tenacious Liberal leader, was held up as the man who would cure all. Some sleuth reporter dug up the fact that Howard had failed his high school maths exam and asked, mischievously, whether this was really the man to turn the economy around. But it had little impact, and that March Howard was elected Prime Minister; he was to remain in office for almost twelve years.

But it seemed that, more than the economy, it was Keating's personality that had lost Labor the election. Most conceded that he was smart; it just appeared that everyone, either with a glint of affection or a scowl of disdain, invariably referred to him as 'that arrogant bastard'.

This wasn't altogether unjustified. He was famous, for example, for having grievously breached protocol by putting his arm around Queen Elizabeth II in 1992. Depending on one's political persuasion, this either horrified or delighted people – being interpreted as a villainous sign of disrespect to Her Majesty or as a signal to Old Lizzy of Australia's modern egalitarianism and national independence.

But Keating's contempt for political peers was generally considered to be extreme. This was quite an achievement in a country where the federal parliament often resembles a workingman's bar-room and where, for example, the Democrats, the most respectable party in politics (equating roughly to the UK Liberal Democrats), ran their 1996 federal campaign under the slogan of 'Keep the Bastards [i.e. politicians] honest'.

To illustrate Keating's obvious disdain for his fellow politicians, the opposition once circulated a list of over fifty terms he had used to describe them in parliament. They included 'harlots, sleazebags, piece of criminal garbage, scumbag, pigs, perfumed gigolos and stunned mullets'. He chided one member by saying that 'like a dog, he returns to his own vomit' and equated being chastised by another opponent as 'like being flogged with warm lettuce'. It was fair to say that he was a man to make a mark, and had few friends on the other side of the political divide.

Given his widely credited intelligence, Keating really should have learnt a few more tricks from his predecessor Bob Hawke, one of the stellar figures in Australian political history. Hawke was clearly destined for great things from an early age, not so much by winning a Rhodes scholarship to Oxford in the 1960s, but by spending his time there so well that he secured the Guinness world record for drinking the fastest yard of ale (eleven seconds). This record stood for many years, and greatly enhanced his prospects of reaching high political office in Australia.

He smartly turned his drinking celebrity to great advantage. When elected Prime Minister in 1980, he declared publicly that to better dedicate himself to the onerous demands of serving the nation he would give up the booze for his period in office. 'No greater sacrifice', thought the common man, and it went down a storm.

He too had his wisecracks. On the new Prime Minister, he once remarked: 'John Howard makes the *Kama Sutra* look positively meagre. I mean, he's got so many positions you can't keep up with him.' And the morning of Australia's famous victory in the America's Cup yacht race in 1983, he came on national television to announce that 'any employer who sacks a worker for taking a day off today is a bum'. In Australia, he's still considered a legend.

But Hawke was the exception. Many of the more influential Australian prime ministers since the war, such as Menzies, Fraser and Whitlam, had a strongly patrician, if not arrogant, air, and Keating was only following in their mould. Indeed, it could be argued that Keating's rejection by the electorate had some parallels with that of his ill-fated Labor predecessor, Gough Whitlam: both were too progressive for such a staunchly conservative country.

Australia is not the land of Ned Kelly rebels and live-and-let-live settlers toughened up by years in the bush, as Lawson's writings might have one believe. It never was, not even in Lawson's time when, as now, the vast majority of the population were urban, ocean-side dwellers living along what is now termed the Boomerang coast, which stretches from Adelaide in South Australia to Brisbane in Queensland. And why would it be, in a country that has enjoyed one of the world's highest standards of living over the last century and where the overriding aspiration remains to own one's own 'place'? These are hardly conditions that create a breeding ground for political radicals. Life's just too cosy.

And it was for that very reason that so many backpackers quickly fell in love with Australia and began looking around for ways to stay.

Fifty Years On: VP Day, 1995

Australians might appear laconic and laid back, but there's one thing that they take very seriously, and that's their Diggers.

I came to realise this soon after my arrival, in August 1995, on the fiftieth anniversary of VP, or Victory in the Pacific, Day. It might have been five decades since the end of the Second World War, but clearly memories were still quite raw.

The two world wars, which came as Australia was still only just emerging from its status as a colony, played a huge part in defining Australia's sense of self. Although federation from Britain was achieved in 1901, it is commonly recognised that only on the beaches of Gallipoli in 1915 did Australia truly become a nation. The Second World War, and in particular the war in the Pacific, further widened the link with Britain, as Australia turned to America for military protection. But perhaps the strongest badge of identity to come out of the wars was the icon of the Aussie 'Digger', which soon came to be seen as the embodiment of all that was best in the national character.

The 'Digger' character that emerged from the goldfields of Victoria and Western Australia in the nineteenth century came into his own in Gallipoli: falling by the thousand, Australians proved themselves to be among the finest soldiers in the Commonwealth. Outstandingly courageous (and resourceful – an Australian at Gallipoli, for example, invented the periscope rifle), on several occasions Ellis Ashmead-Bartlett, the English *Daily Telegraph* war correspondent at Gallipoli, reported seeing Anzacs splashing about in the sea as shrapnel and shells exploded all around them. General Sir John Maxwell, the British commanding officer in Egypt, wrote privately in October 1915, six months after the Gallipoli landings, that 'the [Australian] men are splendid as fighters, the best the world has seen! No words can over-praise them.'

But Australia paid a high price for its involvement in the Great War, which was, after all, fought mainly in the distant battlefields of Europe. From a population of less than five million, 300,000 men enlisted, of whom over 60,000 were killed and 156,000 wounded, gassed or taken prisoner. With two out of every three Australian becoming a casualty, the country proportionately suffered far more than any other in the war. But despite the appalling number of dead and wounded, the First World War showed the entire Empire that Australia was no longer a convict dumping ground for the dregs of civilised society but rather that it was now a country of undaunted and resilient individuals.

With the Second World War, the conflict came directly to the continent. Darwin, Townsville, Port Hedland, Wyndham and Broome were bombed by Japanese aircraft, killing hundreds. Papua New Guinea, Australia's sole protectorate, was invaded by land troops, and three Japanese midget submarines even breached the defences to Sydney harbour to sink an old ship hulk. Australia's sense of itself as being a faraway, unassailable place was dashed as the threat of a Japanese invasion became ever more real. Australia now, very realistically, came to understand that Britain could not be relied upon to protect it. And as the Pacific war escalated, it quickly became apparent that Australia's interests were much better served by a closer alliance with its neighbour across the Pacific Ocean, the United States of America.

If Gallipoli is the lasting folk memory of the First World War, it is the Japanese prisoner of war camps that are the visceral, emotional legacy of the Second World War in Australia. Even fifty years later, the horrific treatment meted out to Australia's Diggers – where, as is well known, for every sleeper laid on the notorious Burma-Thailand railway an allied prisoner died – still rankled.

Given the very significant anniversary, huge media attention was paid that year to John Major's reception of the Japanese Prime Minister in London. In protest at the lack of an official Japanese apology or compensation for the camps' survivors, former POWs orchestrated a solemn display of disrespect by turning their backs on the Japanese leader as he passed by. This was in England; but in Australia, even in 1995, the virulent sense of outrage towards Japan was startling.

A few days before that fiftieth VP Day, I heard a dignified and measured voice come on the radio as I pottered around my flat in Waverley. The Diggers, he said, had been sent to Singapore in 1942 even through the government knew there was little chance of holding off the Japanese advance. They were effectively sacrificed to afford Australia more time to build up its defences and get on a better war footing. But the men accepted the need for sacrifice in war, and they went. Most of them were imprisoned by the Japanese, and more than half of them never returned. The remainder, fifty years on, have still not received meaningful compensation from the government. It had been a government decision in 1942 to send those men, and now these men needed more medical attention than others in their age group. The government was therefore responsible for providing these men with financial compensation to pay for their care. At the conclusion of the interview, the speaker was named as the president of the New South Wales prisoner-of-war association.

Given many Australians' experience during the war, it's hardly surprising that anti-Asian feeling still runs deep in the country. In those few years, Pauline Hansen's openly anti-Aborigine and anti-Asian One Nation party was rapidly gaining ground. Even among many moderate Australians, almost thirty years after the removal of the 'White Australia' immigration policy, I often heard many anti-Asian 'asides' in relation to new immigrants.

In the Canberra War Museum, which I later visited, a noticeboard asked 'Where were you on VE/VP Day?' Dozens of cards had been pinned up by visitors – some were from ex-serviceman, others from those who'd been children in 1945. One remembered the day vividly as the first time he'd ever seen his father drunk. Another, written by a sailor who'd been in a naval base in Britain on VP Day, told his story briefly. Then, at the side of the card, in heavily scored capital letters, he'd added: 'AND THEY ARE STILL WINNING. THE JAPS ARE VERY CRUEL PEOPLE!'

As noon struck on that VP Day anniversary, the screeching whine of the 'all-clear' siren reverberated throughout the nineteen storeys of the bank.

Although the two-minute silence had been announced earlier, I wasn't prepared for the eerie sound, or the goose-pimples that broke out on my skin as all around me, normally loud and rambunctious employees suddenly turned to stone.

An hour later I caught the memorial parade passing down George Street, Sydney's main thoroughfare. Floats laden with young people in forties suits, overcoats and trilby hats passed by, jiving with each other, bashing away at old black typewriters, or just waving to the crowd.

The old men silently closed off the procession. Most of them, medals pinned to their jackets, sat in wheelchairs or on seats, walking sticks by their side. Distant and rheumy-eyed, they hardly appeared to notice the cheering crowds gathering around in the pleasant winter sunshine. Office workers, out catching a quick lunchtime sandwich, would stop and surreptitiously edge up to the rear of the crowd to gaze at these old men with a respect verging on veneration. Coming from such a notoriously irreverent people, I knew I was seeing something quite special.

Leaving work that evening, I turned into Martin Place expecting to see the normal twilight scene of busy commuters rushing down the wide flight of stairs to take the metro home. But instead that evening I collided with a wall of light so blinding that it made me lurch backwards. A news crew was filming at the side of the Monument to the Unknown Soldier, and two dazzling television lamps cast a buttery light on the lower half of the square. The stone coffin was surrounded by wreaths and tributes; detouring from my usual commuter dash, I walked slowly around its base, reading the inscriptions.

Alongside wreaths from military units and veterans groups, there were several personal bouquets with notes pinned to them written in a faint, shaky hand. Reading them in that eerie light, it was strange to think that a sibling or former sweetheart might still be grieving for someone who had been killed more than half a century before.

I was so absorbed in reading the inscriptions that it was some time before I looked up again from the monument. Steams of commuters were now surging quickly past me and disappearing down through the sunken metro entrance into Martin Place station. Still in a trance, I turned to join them. Going down the steps, I realised that Australia had surprised me once more. It wasn't turning out to be as a sunny and simple a land as I'd expected.

The Australian Backpacker

The term 'backpacker' is a peculiar one in Australia. In my time on the continent, it applied indiscriminately to anyone in the country on a temporary visa, regardless of whether they ever backpacked or not. The tag stuck, even if, as was often the case, the 'backpacker' never ventured further than the Blue Mountains and spent all their time and money drinking in King's Cross or down the Rocks.

These reservations could never be levelled at Rob, who, in my view, was not only the epitome of the Australian 'backpacker', but one of the greats. Although no slouch on the drinking front, Rob had seen more of the continent in his first month by driving his camper-van across to Perth than most 'backpackers' saw in their whole year. But Rob proved his backpacker credentials not so much by his travels as through his natural gifts. Not only was he terrific company, unfailingly well connected and rarely fazed, but he seemed to know how to pick up on every bargain, trick or scam going on at any time.

So although my circle of acquaintances had grown in the months of his absence, I was delighted to hear his familiar lisping voice over the phone just before Christmas, saying that he was back, and asking to kip on my floor for a few days. What had brought him back to Sydney in December, he later explained, was Bondi Beach's famous Christmas Day party.

For such an Australian icon, Bondi can be a real letdown. Its eight-hundred-metre beach is perhaps the least impressive even of the Eastern Beaches, and it certainly can't hold a candle to Manly on Sydney's North Shore. But whatever about its disappointing reality, it still managed to draw thousands of backpackers each year on Christmas Day to its midsummer Yuletide party.

Talking to Rob afterwards, he was clear on the early events of the day: he had acquired a wheelie bin, filled it with beer and ice, and pushed it down to the thronged party on Bondi. He'd then spent much of the day in fine style. Whenever he wanted an icy beer, he simply stretched out his arm and fished it out of the bin.

But it was a long day's drinking under a hot sun, and things soon became fuzzy. He vaguely remembers the fights that broke out that evening along the esplanade between ethnic gangs from western Sydney. But how he came to wake up on the roadside somewhere between Bondi and Surry Hills at 4 AM staring up at the stars – that, he admitted, was quite beyond him.

But soon back on his feet, he was keen to show me some of the interesting tricks he'd picked up on his travels. Perhaps the most useful of these was how to scam free international phone calls.

With email, text messaging and Skype still things of the future, costly telephone calls were then the main means of staying in contact with home. So defrauding phone companies was nothing new. The location of faulty public phones would pass with dizzying speed through the backpacker grapevine, and long queues would soon form outside isolated phone boxes around the city. But Rob's was no ordinary scam, and after exhaustive research around Sydney, he invited me one afternoon to a grubby phone box behind Central Station for a formal demonstration.

Lifting the receiver, he inserted an international phone card and explaining that the method worked on only some phones, he dialled his mother's number in Yorkshire. Then, with the concentration of a safe-cracker, he listened intently to the beeps of the dial tone. At a precise number of beeps, he whipped out the phone card and, his face and shoulders visibly relaxing, began talking with England. At that, I went for a walk.

Rob had an ability that always astounded me. He could talk by phone, quite literally, for hours, and the conversation never seemed to drag. Every evening after his free calls, he would entertain me over drinks with tales from home as fresh in gossip as if he'd just left the pub in Batley, his home town near Leeds. This seemed to act like a double-edged sword for him, because as good as it was to stay in touch with England – most of us rang home only about twice a month – being in such close contact, Rob seemed to miss it all the more, and at times his homesickness was quite palpable.

When Rob found work in a cosmetics warehouse near his home in Surry Hills just after Christmas, his female roommates were delighted. Made-up and perfumed, they would accompany Rob like pretty mafia molls whenever he ventured out to the pub.

It was fortunate that Rob had free access to such pleasant fragrances as he lived in that odd entity, a backpacker warren. From the outside, it looked like any other small, two-bedroom Sydney home. But passing through the doorway, the mattresses, the clothing and the lifeless bodies sprawled around the sitting room soon belied the true nature of the place. When I called over, Rob would introduce me one by one to a steady stream of bodies emerging half-dressed and clearly hungover from each of the various bedrooms.

'Paul, have you met Graham?' he'd ask. 'I wouldn't normally let a bloody shandy-drinking southerner into the house, but we've rent to pay and beggars can't be choosers, eh?' In introducing the characters, Rob would conveniently ignore the fact that rent was normally no more than forty dollars a week, and that Graham would be from nowhere further south than Birmingham.

Given his living conditions, and the penny-pinching ways of most back-packers as they save to go travelling, the extravagance of my housing situation seemed a great distress to Rob. And when I moved into a new flat in Leichhardt, in Sydney's Italian area towards the end of the first year, he could contain himself no longer.

It really was a delightful room, I thought, and well worth the hundred dol-lars' weekly rent. With high, mauve-coloured walls, it was large and mostly empty except for a double mattress, some well-worn clothes and an expanding collection of second-hand books piling up on the floor. Two tall wooden doors led out onto a Perspex-covered balcony, and on winter mornings I'd lie in bed and watch the sunlight stream through the curtainless windows and suffuse the room with a deliciously warm, mauve-tinged mellowness.

But Rob had no time for such fanciness, especially when he found out how much I was paying. One evening, unable to take it any more, he cast his critical eye over the room's acres of empty carpet, and spoke up.

'You do know there's room for two mattresses over there by the window, and you could fit another one over there along the wall,' he said, trying to keep the trace of reprimand out of his voice. When I tried to explain that I liked having a place to read and spend time on my own, he was having none of it.

Living in a crowded house wasn't all bad, he insisted. It only meant that for the sake of your sanity, you had to get out to the pub *every* night of the week, instead of just the normal once every three nights. But with sixty bucks saved off my weekly rent, he reasoned, I'd easily have the ready cash for the extra beers. He kindly offered to organise three more people to share the room. 'So waddya say?' he concluded professionally. 'Just give me the word, and I'll sort it out.'

But each time I'd gently refuse, and Rob would leave the room a bowed man.

In that first year, I spurned the common practice of sharing with only Irish and English backpackers, and once again my new 'roomies' in Leichhardt were all Australian; from Bathhurst and Orange, two country towns in the New South Wales interior. After several years away from home, both studying in university and now working, their ability to live on little more than tap water was truly educational. Our collective weekly shopping run down to Franklin's 'No Frills' supermarket came to just over twenty dollars per person, as two-minute noodles, cheap pasta and vast lumps of artery-clogging cheese became my staple diet for the next five months. The financial budgeting I learnt in that house was worthy of a business degree, and the savings made must have brought forward my departure for Queensland by at least two months.

But whatever economies I made on food shopping were now being safely offset by my spending on alcohol. Several nights a week I would be down the pub with Rob and his coiffured entourage, or with Len, Tom and my bank colleagues, enjoying two-dollar schooners during all-night-long 'happy hour' promotions. After almost ten months in Australia, it was fair to say that I'd long since broken my Confirmation pledge. And the more I found myself being woken up at the terminus by the bus driver, the more I had to admit that I was probably drinking a little too much than was good for me.

Perhaps my sense of being in limbo, and my nervous uncertainty about what I would do if I had to leave the country, go some way to explaining my excessive drinking at this time. Because as the early southern winter months rolled quickly on, I realised that I now had a pressing matter to deal with – namely the impending expiry of my one-year visa.

Like most people coming to Australia on a one-year working-holiday visa, within a short time I was hooked. The lifestyle and opportunities the country offered seemed extraordinary for someone coming from Ireland. I certainly wanted to stay longer than the initial twelve-month visa allowed – if perhaps not for life. The simple question was, how?

It was evident that the days of the ten-quid assisted passage were long gone. Now, without a trade such as carpentry or plumbing, or a degree, with experience, such as engineering or geology, the likelihood of obtaining full residency on a skills basis seemed slim.

Stuck in this bind, many backpackers chose to stay on illegally; something Rob was to do for another three years. The penalty seemed comparatively light: immediate extradition was followed by a five-year ban from the country. But I had no interest in living the uncertain life of an illegal; there had to be other ways. And investigating it more, I quickly learned about some of the smart – and crackpot – ruses backpackers got up to.

One straightforward means, open to those with dual British and Irish citizenships, was to return home at the end of the first year, and then obtain a second visa on their other passport.

Political asylum was a route taken by one Irish girl I met. Declaring that her father's close IRA connections placed her in danger of being kneecapped, if not killed, if she returned to Ireland, she managed to extend her stay for at least another year.

Not given to such extremes, I soon concluded that a de facto visa seemed my best option. At that time, a person had to live with an Australian citizen as a common-law spouse for a minimum of six months before applying. This was a godsend for people on twelve-month visas, as it allowed enough time to find a new friend, platonic or otherwise, to go along with the game.

After the couple went through a lengthy interrogation process with Immigration, the non-Australian national qualified for a two-year working-residency visa on the proviso that the pair continued to live together on a de facto married basis. Many intense – and pretence – romances blossomed; some even lasted. Most couples, however, split up not long after the visa interrogation – although, needless to say, Immigration was always the last to be told.

To pursue this avenue, I reluctantly left Dominique's charming house in Waverley to move in with my Australian girlfriend in the rather rundown, predominantly Asian suburb of Marrickville. Trouble soon reached paradise, however, and even with the carrot of a de facto visa dangling before me, I decided that some things are just not meant to be. It was then that I moved into Leichhardt.

With the 'de facto' now off the table, my visa options seemed exhausted. Although the first mutterings of an economic upturn in Ireland began to filter down to Australia around St Patrick's Day 1996, I wasn't interested in returning yet. Besides, after years in the economic doldrums, it seemed hard to believe. What was there to go back to? A crummy job, awful weather and the familiar humdrum. It seemed to contrast in every way with Australia and my strong thirst for adventure. I desperately wanted to stay.

A chink of light appeared one morning when I lamented my plight to Andy, a Scottish colleague in the bank. 'Aye, but you know there's one loophole they don't tell you about. How do you think I'm still here after two years?' Apply for permanent residency on the skills basis in an offshore Australian embassy before your first visa expired, he told me, and they'll give you a bridging visa while it's being processed. 'Try Auckland,' he suggested, with a smirk. 'With the pile of applications they have there, you never know, it might even be a year before they get to yours.'

Within days, my visa application was off in the post to New Zealand, and then the nervous wait began.

But luck was with me, as in mid-July, only days before my first twelve-month visa was due to expire, my bridging visa came through. Feeling suddenly unburdened, and itching to finally see some more of this vast continent, two weeks later I flew down to Hobart, the chilly state capital of Tasmania.

Tasmania

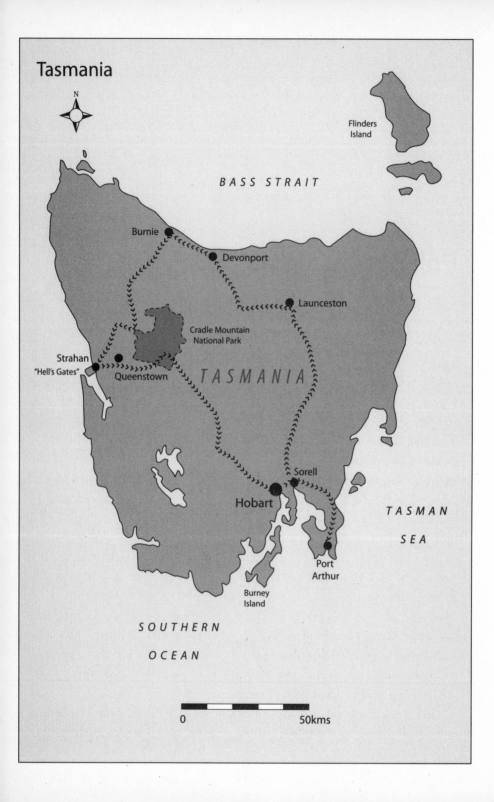

Tasmania

N

Flinders
Island

BASS STRAIT

Burnie

Devonport

Launceston

Cradle Mountain
National Park

Strahan
"Hell's Gates"

Queenstown

T A S M A N I A

Sorell

Hobart

TASMAN

SEA

Port
Arthur

Burney
Island

SOUTHERN

OCEAN

0   50kms

Hobart, Tasmania

On 28 April 1996, a man named Martin Bryant walked into the Broad Arrow Café in Port Arthur in Tasmania. It was a Sunday afternoon, and as usual the old convict tourist site was busy with day-trippers. Finishing his lunch on the outside balcony, Bryant took a semi-automatic shotgun from his sports bag and started firing at the diners around him. Killing and injuring many, Bryant went after those who had scrambled away in panic, firing continually and calmly reloading each weapon as it ran out. With much of the slaughter completed, he then barricaded himself into the nearby home of an elderly couple. The following morning, with the couple lying dead and their house aflame, he was finally captured by the police. The death toll was shocking: more than twenty people had been severely injured, and thirty-five people were dead. It was, up to that time, the largest killing by a lone gunman in modern times.

Australia might be a vast place but with less than twenty million people it's a relatively small community and the country went into a state of deep shock. In the bank, thousands of kilometres away in Sydney, people were deeply affected; their sense of outrage and incomprehension was similar to what followed the Omagh bombing in Northern Ireland in 1998. How could a man with a mild intellectual disability legally acquire automatic and semi-automatic weapons, people asked. And just what made him want to kill so many people out enjoying a normal Sunday outing?

Stricter gun controls for semi-automatic weapons were soon introduced, and capital punishment was hotly discussed in the media and parliament. But, never ones to look on at another bloke's misfortunes, Australians stayed away from the island that year, and Tasmania's tourism sector and general economy were hit badly.

Prompted by a bank colleague recently returned from the island and taking advantage of half-price airfares, that July, less than three months after the Port Arthur killings, I flew down to Tasmania.

In contrast to Sydney's by-now-familiar, pleasant climate, I first saw Tasmania's dunny-brown landscape through a frosted aircraft window as we landed in Hobart on a cold, late-midwinter afternoon.

Although Tasmania is about the size of Ireland and has a population of a million and a half people, Hobart International Airport at that time was little more than a large tin shed. Seeing passengers being greeted by beaming, ruddy-faced friends and relatives dressed in thick woollen sweaters, I knew that I was arriving into a small, close-knit community. So reminiscent was it of a scene from an Irish country-bus station that I felt my first twinge of homesickness since leaving Ireland more than a year before.

As I'd booked my hostel by phone, I was a little surprised when the airport minibus pulled up outside a pub festooned with Guinness and neon shamrocks signs. 'Come on, mate. Here ya are,' the bus driver hollered as he threw me my backpack. 'The best Irish pub in Hobart. Your hostel's upstairs. You won't have far to stagger tonight, now will ya?'

The male dorm I was shown to was the usual scene of devastation and strong bodily odours. Dumping my backpack, I surveyed the room. I saw on one bed an odd-looking pamphlet and, intrigued, flicked it over. An official British government publication read 'on the effects of' some tortuous scientific term explained in brackets by the three letters 'LSD'. Carefully replacing it, I went out for a walk.

Hobart at eight-thirty on a Saturday night was like a ghost town, and Salamanca, the nineteenth-century old-port area, was like a foggy scene from a Sherlock Holmes murder tale. The sinister atmosphere made me uneasy, and I soon returned to the hostel in search of company.

Unlike most Australian hostels, which are generally of an excellent standard, this one looked shoddy and rundown. The common room was a rag-bag of battered furniture and broken appliances. Apart from the assortment of threadbare brown armchairs, an antique, grease-discoloured oven sat in the corner beside a toaster machine whose door hung on by a single hinge. Although invitingly warm, the room was empty except for two young back-packers and a slightly built, middle-aged man sitting on his own. His eyes darted nervously around the room trying unobtrusively to take in every sign of activity. Neatly dressed in his beige v-neck pullover and slacks, he looked distinctly out of place in a backpacker hostel; from the glances of the two other people there, it was obvious that he was an eccentric, and well to be avoided.

But as I sat down to look at the Australian swimmer Kieran Perkins's gold medal victory in the 1500 metres Olympic freestyle final, the older man silently sat down on the armchair beside me.

'A wonderful performance, wasn't it?' he observed. His manner was so timid and unassuming that I found it difficult not to have compassion for him.

After his daring ice-breaker, he gathered the courage to enquire in what professional sector I was employed.

'Currently I'm in the banking area,' I replied.

Not picking up on my wry tone in response to his oddly formal language, he was quick to explain that his career had been one 'operating in the insurance/pensions sector, so to speak. This experience,' he told me, had made him 'very concerned about the current imbalance in the national demographic structure and its imminent impact on social services.'

Then he abruptly changed tack. 'I'm a reformed alcoholic, you know. In the eighties I'd drink up to six bottles of cheap wine a day. On account of this, I lost my job and my family.' His eldest son, he said, looking at me as directly as his inordinate shyness permitted, was probably about the same age as I was.

It was when in recovery, he elaborated, that his psychologist had diagnosed him as bipolar. 'Bipolar dysfunctionality – the very same disorder King George the Third suffered from,' he whispered. 'You might have seen the recent film about him, *The Madness of King George*. They used a different term for it in those days.' This diagnosis had aroused his curiosity about a story his grand-mother had told him as a boy, and he had spent the previous three years researching it.

The very same King George, he said, had fathered an illegitimate son by an Irish lady in the early 1800s. When the boy was eleven, the king, to rid himself of this inconvenience, had sent him off in the care of a tutor to the new Crown colony of Australia, and he had wound up in Van Diemen's Land. The child's surname was changed he said, spelling out the surname letter by letter to me. And this boy, his grandmother had recounted, was her great-grandfather.

This story to him came as some relief, he continued, as it helped to explain that the mental depression that had afflicted him for so many years was genetic and could be traced back to his royal lineage.

With his new love, whom he had met in the local library, he was now intent 'with our small assets to restore our family name'. He alluded to the recent woes of the British royal family (Charles and Diana had only finalised their divorce two weeks before) and I realised that by 'our family' he meant the House of Windsor. How he was going to accomplish the restoration of the dynasty he didn't specify, and after a few minutes I excused myself from his company and palpable loneliness, and returned to the dorm.

Back in the empty room, I leaned my back against the door and looked up at the grimy ceiling. I'd been here less than five hours, and already Tasmania was proving to be a strange place. Anything could be possible in a land like this. So much so that the odd story I'd just heard could very well be true.

I needed a drink. Downstairs, a few minutes later, an ex-miner named James introduced himself to me as I stood at the bar. He'd just seen me in the common room. 'Odd bloke, that. Lonely old bugger, eh?'

James had just spent the last year – and more than thirty thousand dollars – in Europe and was now meandering his way back to Sydney. He was to entertain me with tall tales for the rest of the night. He'd loved Ireland, he said. But he had some bad memories, as just before leaving for home his camera and all the photos he'd taken on his travels were stolen. I sympathised but as I placed a fresh Guinness in front of him his pain seemed to ease.

'Hey, here's one I heard from some old-timers in this tiny place up the coast.' He looked apologetic even before he spoke.

'OK, here goes. Why is Port Arthur like the Antarctic?'

I shook my head nervously. He lowered his voice to a whisper. 'Because they're both minus thirty-five!'

There were a few seconds of awkward silence; thirty-five people killed so recently, and so near to where we were now, was not something to joke about lightly. 'Yeah, I know, sick. But that's one these old-timers told me. Can you believe it?'

A few hours later, two guys walked in and James introduced us. One, a baggy-eyed Dutchman, proved to be the inquisitive pamphlet-reader in my dorm. He'd come to nearby Tasmania, he explained, after a spot of bother with some drug dealers in Amsterdam. He was now selling hi-fi equipment around the island out of the back of a van, aided by the Irish guy beside him. We quickly investigated our degrees of separation, and in true Irish style discovered we had grown up within a mile of each other in Dublin. Like long-lost cousins, we called for a round of drinks. A long night was had.

Port Arthur

Early the following morning, still groggy, I boarded the ten-seater minibus of the Convict Coaches bus fleet bound for Port Arthur. The convict site, my guidebook said, was only about an hour from Hobart, and for the first few kilometres I looked out over the landscape wondering if I'd spot any interesting wildlife. I was particularly intrigued by the stuffed versions of both the Tasmanian devil and the Tasmanian tiger I'd seen in Hobart's threadbare museum the day before.

Tasmanian Tigers resembled hyenas and from the dark stripes down their flanks one can see how they got their name. But I knew there was no hope of spotting one: the last tiger had died in Hobart zoo in 1936. Blurry black-and-white photographs in the museum showed mounds of their carcasses stacked up after hunting expeditions and farmers' roundups. There have been some unconfirmed sightings of the animal since the 1930s, and some hope remains, as parts of the island have scarcely been explored. But it is probable that the Tasmanian tiger has now gone the way of the dodo.

The Tasmanian devil, however, is still quite abundant. It is a ferocious animal, about the size of a small dog. Equipped with an impressive set of predators' teeth, they generally live on rodents, though they often kill cats and other larger animals. Although I failed to spot one on the bus journey, I was rewarded the following day when I saw one of their corpses, a roadkill, near Port Arthur.

Our journey stretched beyond an hour as we made various detours to shops and a medical clinic to either drop off or pick up parcels and letters. After the final stop, the driver climbed back heavily into his seat and, turning around, apologised for the delays. The tension in his voice was at odds with his evidently kindly disposition. He held the licence for the postal run between Hobart and Port Arthur, he explained, and was just picking up a few parcels.

Things hadn't been so good lately, he said gravely. Between my fare and the few dollars he got for the postal run, he'd only just cover his petrol costs for the day.

'It's been like that ever since what happened in April. I can count on one hand the people I've carried in each of the weeks since then. Getting up at five in the morning to make two or three bucks doesn't really seem worth it any more. At least not at my age.'

Now in his early sixties, he had worked most of his life for the post office. He'd only taken up the van run a few years before, 'for a little extra cash and something to do'. But this week, he said, would be the last week of his working life. He'd already sold the van – at a loss – but between his post office pension and a little savings, he and his wife would be able to manage if they lived quietly.

'Other places are feeling it too,' he added, meaning the few small shops and the bar in the Port Arthur site. 'Their business has virtually dried up as well. They're all afraid they might have to close. And then God knows what they'll do.'

It was another twenty minutes before we negotiated the last of the windy country lanes, and the driver finally pulled in to the side of the road. Pointing down a small track, he told me it would bring me to the hostel. He came down to the site at ten every morning, so he might see me the next day or later in the week. If the warden wasn't inside, he told me to just make myself at home, and that she'd be down later in the day. And with that, and a friendly nod, he set off back to Hobart like a fretting coachman anxious to make a quick escape from Dracula's castle.

Apprehensively, I carried my bags down to the hostel. The main door was open, and entering its cold hall I felt like I was boarding a creaking *Marie Celeste*, abandoned in the mid-Atlantic wastes. I wandered through every room and didn't meet a soul. I peered out a window at the convict site a hundred metres down the hill. A lacerating wind carried a drenching rain directly up from the Antarctic. It was certainly uninviting. But wrapping up warmly, I went out again and made my way down to the seemingly deserted heritage site.

It was eerie entering the site on that out-of-season Monday afternoon. The Broad Arrow Café, where Bryant had killed his first victims, was still boarded up, and walking the tarmac to the ticket office my skin crawled to think that less than three months before, the surface below my feet was probably covered with blood, and the dying bodies of visitors to Port Arthur, just like me.

A middle-aged woman behind the counter was talking with a nervous rapidity to two French visitors, almost as if she was trying to cut off any chance of them asking questions. When I glanced up to take my ticket moments later, her eyes seemed to have a look of animal terror. I left the office quickly, and it was only when I was outside that I noticed the message printed on the back of the information leaflet. I read it as I walked across the wet lawn, past a freshly cut wooden cross, and entered the ruins of the main prison building.

As a result of the recent tragedies, it explained, 'many staff and residents have lost family members and friends and are still deeply distressed. . . . You can help staff and convey your respect for their grief and privacy by not asking them to provide details about the recent tragedy. . . . Thank you for your understanding.'

At its height in the 1830s, Port Arthur was inhabited by two thousand convicts and one thousand of their keepers with their families. Even now, their presence is almost palpable among the prison ruins nestling so incongruously in this natural idyll. It seems now as peaceful as any abandoned, dark-age monastery site. The most visible physical reminder of the site's past is the three-storey façade of the old red-brick prison building, whose gutted window-frames seem to stare out from on high like sunken eye-sockets.

The free settlers had no love for the memory of the place, or for their convict history, and after the end of transportation in 1853 they wasted no time in changing the colony's name from Van Diemen's Land to its current name, Tasmania. The old penitentiary was also gutted by fire several decades afterwards – whether accidentally or otherwise is still unknown. But regardless of the neglect and the attempted oblivion, Port Arthur retains a striking, indelible atmosphere. Robert Hughes was so overwhelmed by his first visit to the site that he was inspired to write his monumental history of Australian convictism, *The Fatal Shore* (a copy of which I later picked up in a secondhand bookshop in Launceston).

Watching the awestruck visitors wandering in a daze around the grounds, I realised that what I was feeling was commonly shared. On a tour of the penitentiary, given later that evening, the guide told us about two visitors who on separate tours had gone missing. After a search, both had been found huddled in the foetal position in a particular cell, crying and whimpering. Later, each explained that when they'd entered that cell, they'd been suddenly overwhelmed by a sense of black despair and had curled up in a ball in the corner, feeling utterly helpless. The guide pointed out that in that cell, the only prisoner who'd succeeded in committing suicide in the penitentiary had hanged himself by the bars of the window. Such was the dark atmosphere of the place that not one of our group appeared in the least surprised.

In nineteenth-century folklore, Van Diemen's Land was known as the worst place on God's earth, and in this case the ballads were not far wrong. Through the vicious discipline of the first commandant, Charles Booth O'Hara, the penal colony very much lived up to the aspiration of Governor Arthur that Port Arthur would take 'the vengeance of the Law to the very limits of human endurance'. Convicted prisoners, after spending months on overcrowded hulks on English and Irish estuaries, and then enduring pestilent months at sea, found themselves washed up here.

Most of them ended up doing hard labour in icy waters up to their chest, hewing and lugging trees to provide for the burgeoning British navy. Inevitably, this hard labour caused many broken arms and legs, and due to the ignorance of the prison doctors, who seemed unaware that broken bones could be reset, many convicts had their limbs amputated. Malnourished, and working in such severe conditions, many of the convicts inevitably succumbed to pneumonia and other diseases, and died within a short time of arrival.

But in some respects, these convicts were fortunate in comparison to those who ended up in the penitentiary. The penal system was the brainchild of a man named Jeremy Bentham, who believed, quite radically, that jails should not just be a place of punishment, but also a place of reform. Recalcitrant men and women had to be broken in spirit for them to see the errors of their ways. Only then could they become truly penitent for their sins. And the way to break their spirit was not by physical punishment but by sensory deprivation.

Wild grass and bulrush leaves were scattered on the floors, and the guards wore rubber-soled shoes so that their pacing could not be heard by the prisoners, who were locked in their single cells for twenty-three hours each day and kept in almost complete mental isolation. Even when they were called out from their cell – and always by a number – for exercise, or even for religious service, a hood was placed over their heads to prevent them seeing, or being seen by, their fellow convicts.

Dehumanised, many prisoners ended up in the asylum that was soon constructed beside the main prison building. The guards checked prisoners' cells every half an hour to prevent suicides, which would undoubtedly have been rife otherwise. Indeed, Robert Hughes notes that in the 1870s, twenty years after the ending of transportation, 'Tasmania had more paupers, lunatics, orphans and invalids than South Australia and Queensland combined, concentrated in a population less than half of theirs'.

Among those thrown up on this fatal shore were the Young Ireland leaders after the 1848 rising was defeated. Several of them were to have distinguished careers after their release. Perhaps the most notable was Gavin Duffy, who became Prime Minister of the state of Victoria in 1871. His cottage still stands: at the time of my visits, it was painted an incongruously cheerful orangey-yellow on the hillside above the main settlement. He was the only leader who refused to give his bond of obedience to the Governor and swore that if he had the opportunity, he would do all in his power to escape. As a result, the governor assigned him a cottage where he read and wrote and raised fowl and grew vegetables. But even that building has its ominous associations: it was there that many visitors sheltered from Bryant's murderous spree that April.

I spent my two long days in Port Arthur roaming the empty country roads. Occasionally I'd find myself on a hillside overlooking the ocean; gazing out, I'd imagine the creaking convict ships arriving in after their long voyages bearing their wretched human cargo. Point Puer (which the locals pronounce Point Poor), the site of the boys' reformatory prison, is visible across the inlet. Their wretched lives were made part of Australian folklore in Marcus Clark's celebrated novel, *The Term of His Natural Life*. Many, however, were taught a trade, and they were often materially better off than they would have been as street thieves and beggars in Britain. Looking across at the island, where hundreds of the brutalised convicts had been buried, I'd wonder at the life of the island keeper, a convict, living with those corpses and the scarifying climate he had to endure night after night.

In the late afternoons I'd wind my way back up to the empty hostel and the warm stove which the warden would have lit a few hours before. Feeding the stove from the woodpile, I'd cook some hot food, and write letters, or my diary. Afterwards, reading Tolstoy, it was hard not to feel as if, along with Levin and Anna Karenina, I was the last person left in this cold, cold world.

On my last evening, just before the light finally drained out of the sky, I walked down to the narrow cross by the grassy harbour edge and read the names of the thirty-five victims who had been alive just three months before. The wood-lettering was still fresh and rough-cut. But I didn't stay long. It was bitterly cold, and I soon felt frozen to the bone. Walking back up the hill to the hostel, I realised that after only two days in this intense atmosphere, I felt emotionally numb.

The next morning, when the minibus sounded its horn from the roadside, I was long since ready, and I climbed on board. Rarely have I felt such relief at the idea of returning to the ordinariness of daily life. I've travelled widely. I've visited six continents. But still, for me, Port Arthur stands as a place apart. I don't know if tormented souls roam any part of this earth, but if they do, it's surely in that desolate, windswept site at the far end of the world.

The North of the Island

Tasmania is often considered the Little England of Australia. This is something I appreciated all the more the following day on the bus to Launceston, Tasmania's second largest town, which lies at the confluence of the Tamar and the North and South Esk rivers, towards the north of the island. The architecture, people's polite manners, the pretty countryside, and the area's quaintness all seemed to spring straight out of a Beatrix Potter story. Reading Yeats's exquisite poetry on the bus only added to the sense of rural charm. But then another grainy Tasmanian encounter intervened.

'I've to get my son away from that woman!' I heard a man scream. 'You gotta help me get my kid back, for the love of Jesus!' A dishevelled passenger in his late thirties was screeching frantically into his mobile phone just a few rows in front of me. As the bus was almost empty, his desperate pleas were very audible to all on board.

He called the offices of several local social services as he'd gotten wind that his estranged wife had brought their son from her home in Victoria down to live in Tasmania. He had been tipped off that his son had been moved to somewhere near Launceston. He'd flown down the previous day from Victoria and was now on his way north. He had to get an address, he yelled down the phone. His wife had a barring order on him, but he still had legal access to the child.

'But they're both junkies, for Christ's sake. I saw the place they lived in in Victoria. There were needles lying all around the place; the house was like a bloody pigsty. That's no place for my son to grow up in!' He was nearly out of his mind with desperation. 'My son!' he screamed. 'My baby son!' But despite his impassioned pleas, he didn't seem to make much headway. What he did in Launceston, I don't know.

The weather was so wretched in Launceston that after dinner I suggested to two others backpackers that we dart through the downpour from the hostel to the nearby pub. Minutes later, tucking into our first beer, we got better acquainted. The first of my two companions was a rather upper-class young English backpacker. He began telling us almost immediately about the stress his diary was causing him.

'I'm on a five-month trip round Australia,' he explained in his plumy voice. 'I start university in October. I've already been to Sydney and Melbourne – they were great. But you see I'm trying to keep this diary so I can show people back home, especially my mum and dad, because, well' – at this point he reddened a little – 'well . . . because they kinda paid for the trip.'

'I write it up at the end of every day,' he continued. 'But it's so frustrating because all these places are so amazing, and all I seem to write are "the mountains were brilliant" or "the ocean was gorgeous" or "the sunset was superb" and then I seem to run out of adjectives, and when I read over it everywhere sounds more or less the same. I want to tell everyone that these places are *brilliant*, and instead it just sounds almost silly. It's really doing my head in.' A little embarrassed at his sudden outburst, he hid behind his glass and sipped his beer.

I felt myself to be almost an expert in the matter, as I'd kept travel diaries for years. With a flagrant disregard for the state of the rainforests, I was to add another dozen notebooks to that collection while in Australia. This was nothing unusual: diary-writing seemed endemic among backpackers in Australia. Walk into a café or stroll around a historical monument, and you were sure to trip over some budding Marco Polo, journal open, pen poised, pondering their next profound observation.

Backpacker diaries are often voluminous. Without the structure of a daily working or student life, and battered by wave after wave of new thoughts and experiences, the floodgates fly open to one's sense of wonder at the world. These same gates unfortunately are often slammed shut when back in the familiar mundanity of home, just as experiences often lose their magic when one attempts to describe them to family and friends.

The dilemma posed that evening had intrigued me for some time: what exactly should you record in a travel diary? What details merit inclusion?

Mae West, with her usual wit, had once advised: 'Keep a diary and one day it'll keep you!' Samuel Johnson, the man who descended on the Hebrides with equipment to measure the dimensions of the terrain, was of another opinion: 'Every man's life is of importance to himself. Do not omit painful casualties, or unpleasing passages, they make the variegation of existence. . . . That remembrance which is not pleasant may be useful. There is however an intemperate attention to slight circumstances which is to be avoided, lest a great part of life be spent in writing the history of the rest.'

I came across an extreme case of this last point, and a common backpacker vice, on the Ko San road in Bangkok the following year. Struggling over her open diary, I saw a German girl finally turn to her boyfriend and ask him a question I didn't understand. His reply, I did. *'Corn Flakes mit milch.'* *'Ah ja!'* she exclaimed in triumph, and began scribbling once again in her journal. This level of detail – what you had for breakfast – did seem to me excessive.

I thought I'd found the key when reading the journal of Annie Baxter Dawbin, a fiery English woman who'd spent several years in Australia in the nineteenth century, which I'd picked up in Town Hall library in Sydney. 'Now altho' I may choose to show my ideas to anybody,' she wrote in the middle of her always eventful life, 'still I would not, could not, write them for a person's inspection. I have always considered this to be one of the chief beauties of a journal.'

I wanted to suggest to this very likeable English lad that there's a lot more to write about than mountains, landscapes and sunsets. But it seemed that this was something he would have to find out for himself. So I simply listened to him as the rain beat down loudly on the roof above us and drank my beer.

The pub was now filling up, and soon we got chatting to some locals. Almost inevitably, the conversation turned to the topic hanging in the air during my whole visit: Bryant and the Port Arthur killings. Like people in mourning, locals were hesitant to talk, but once they opened up, their feelings poured out.

'Normally,' one of them told us, 'I'd visit the site three or four times a year, just for a day out. It's such a beautiful spot. But not this year.' Why, I asked, as it seemed the people there needed visitors now more than ever? 'It just wouldn't be right,' he replied. 'Most people in the island feel that way.'

'I dunno,' his friend chipped in. 'It'd feel kinda disrespectful to go there so soon. Almost like you were gawking at the place, like it was some sort of show or something.' They talked, and I listened, and soon I felt clammy with shame.

Despite appearances on the map, Tasmania is almost as far from mainland Australia as Ireland is from France, and it takes more than ten hours for the regular ferry from Melbourne to reach the northern port of Devonport. After Launceston, I had come to this town at the tip of the island to catch the three-times-weekly bus service to Strahan, the only town on the west coast. But it was midwinter, and with so few tourists on the island, the bus scheduled to leave the following day had less than the minimum requirement of two passengers, and had been cancelled. I was left with no option but to hire a car for the next morning.

Everywhere in town seemed booked out in anticipation of the ferry's arrival that night, and I felt lucky to snag the last bed in the third hostel I checked. But the crossing was later cancelled due to bad weather, and I found myself once again spending a night in an almost deserted guesthouse. My room was bitterly cold, and I lay shivering in my light sleeping bag trying to sleep as a violent thunderstorm crashed about outside my window.

Creeping into an unlocked dorm, I swiped some spare blankets from an open dresser and returned to my room. Unable to sleep, I sat wrapped up in blankets on my bed like a Red Indian for most of the night, staring out at the flashing blue lightning, lost in thoughts about my solitary trip around this strange island.

Hell's Gates

In 1642 Abel Tasman named the land he had newly discovered at the base of the southern continent after his patron, the Governor-General of the Dutch East Indian company, Anthony Van Diemen. In doing so, he was unaware that it was an island, and for most of the seventeenth century maps depicted Van Diemen's Land as a large bump on the southern coastline of the continent. But twelve thousand years ago, those maps would have been accurate, because it was only at the end of the last Ice Age, as the oceans rose, that the land bridge to the continent disappeared. This not only created the island of Tasmania but also established a new race, the Tasmanian Aborigines, who were the only inhabitants of the island until the arrival of the Europeans.

The Tasmanians were distinct from their mainland counterparts: they were physically stronger but less culturally developed. Tasmanian women shaved their hair close to their head while the men wore theirs in long ringlets smeared in grease and cut scar lines on their abdomens, arms and shoulders for decoration. The Tasmanians were ignorant of the art of fire-making and always carried a smouldering stick on their migrations. They also did not possess that seemingly quintessential Aborigine tool, the boomerang.

But the lives of the estimated four thousand Tasmanian Aborigines changed irrevocably when the first whites arrived in 1793 to hunt seal and whale in the Bass Strait between Tasmania and Australia. Among their first acts was to attack the Tasmanians and to carry off their woman to the Furneux Islands to act as domestic and sex slaves. The founding of the British colony in

1804 only escalated the violence, as settlers – mostly convicts and ticket-of-leave men (convicts released on parole) – freely hunted down and shot the natives and raped the women. Atrocities were commonplace. Robert Hughes, for example, reports a not unusual case where convicts sliced the ear off a captured Aborigine and forced him to eat it.

Understandably, the Tasmanians reacted with a degree of violence, occasionally killing whites and spearing cattle and sheep. This outraged the English, and it was decided that the aboriginal population, despite the fact that it was now diminishing rapidly, posed a threat to the colony. They had to be removed wholesale from the island – by one means or another.

Governor Arthur, adopting sound imperial logic, provided the solution in 1830 with the now notorious 'Black Line'. Collecting together three thousand men – just about every available man in the colony, including convicts and Aborigine trackers – he arrayed them in a line linking one coast to the other. They then set off to trawl the island south to north with the aim of capturing all the remaining Aborigines.

But they met with little success. During daylight, the clanking of their steel equipment and the creaking of their leather gave the Aborigines good warning of their approach. At night, as the whites got drunk by their open fires, the Aboriginal families, intimately familiar with the terrain, simply slipped through the string of lights back into the other half of the island. After a complete scouring of the island, the Black Line netted a total of two Aborigine captives.

But the colonialists were relentless, and there was no escape for the Aborigines. If they surrendered (and survived), they would be removed from their homeland to one of the exposed islands off Tasmania. To a nomadic people, especially one with such a spiritual link to the land, this was a form of death. Consequently, most chose to hold out and die in the bush rather than be forced from their sacred homeland.

But in despair, they gradually brought fewer children into this suddenly darkened world, and the population shrunk quickly. The half-caste children born of Aborigines raped by whites were usually killed at birth by the shamed tribe. The raped gin (female Aborigine) was then considered unclean by her people and another child-bearer was removed from the tribe. On occasion, even a pure Aboriginal baby was killed by its parents as it slowed down or endangered the tribe in their perpetual movement over the island as they attempted to evade capture.

The whites achieved their goal of removing the natives mainly thanks to Aborigines who tracked or enticed in their last remaining kinsmen. Truganini (or Trucanini), perhaps the most famous of these collaborators, was a young gin captured in 1828 aged then about eighteen. Why she helped the whites is a mystery, as she had no reason to love them. Robert Hughes describes her as 'very small, only about 4 feet 3 inches in height, and [with] pronounced curly whiskers; in other respects, all whites agreed, she was remarkably attractive – for an Aborigine. As a child, she had seen her mother stabbed to death in a night raid by whites; later, a sealer named John Baker had kidnapped two of her tribal sisters and her pure-blood sister, Moorina, and taken them into slavery. Her stepmother was abducted by . . . convict mutineers . . . and must have died as they were seeking China'. In 1828, when Truganini was in a boat with several Aborigines crossing from the mainland to Bruny island, the two convict oars-men suddenly stopped and threw the tribesmen overboard. When the Aborigines tried to grab the side of the boat to climb back in, the convicts hacked off their hands and left them to drown. They then rowed Trucanini to shore and raped her.

By 1834, all the remaining Aborigines (one hundred and thirty-five from an estimated four thousand less than four decades before) had been captured and exiled to Flinders Island, a barren, windswept rock in the Bass Straits. In captivity, they began to die rapidly with what anthropologists would later call 'stomach sickness'; when primitive people lose the will to live, they can simply pine away, without any diagnosable illness.

By 1837, the surviving forty-seven Aborigines were transferred to Oyster Cove, just south of Hobart, where most became prostitutes or alcoholics. For official engagements, they were dressed up and paraded around like circus attractions. Ironically, in 1876 Truganini was the last full-blooded Tasmanian Aborigine to die; with her death, the extermination of the pure-blood Tasmanian Aborigines was complete.

Leaving Devonport the following morning, I drove through the isolated western half of the island, where many of those doomed Aborigines had sought refuge a century and a half earlier. Travelling along, I wondered at what black thoughts must have gone through their minds as they fled over these wild mountains and forests, attempting, in vain, to escape their ultimate slaughter by the white settlers. This island seemed to have endless ghosts that had yet to be lain to rest.

Most of Tasmania's one and a half million people live in the eastern half of the island in two clusters, near Hobart or Launceston. The rest of the island is not only scarcely inhabited but almost inaccessible. Strahan, my destination, could only be reached by sea up to 1932 before the road I was now travelling on was constructed over the mountains.

Arriving in the early afternoon, I soon found myself in the small museum on Macquarie Harbour alongside the few scattered houses and shops that make up the hamlet of Strahan. Tasmania was the scene of deep conflicts between loggers and environmentalists in the 1970s and early 1980s – which were only resolved in 1983 when Bob Hawke declared much of the island national heritage parkland.

This was ironic, considering that it was the abundance of Huon Pine, then considered perhaps the world's best wood for ship-building, which caused Strahan to be founded as a penal colony. No freemen could have been enticed to the brutal beast-of-burden logging work here in this remotest of locations, in the wettest climate in Australia. The only solution was slave labour – or a penal colony.

The locals in the pub in Launceston had told me that in convict times Strahan had been even grimmer than Port Arthur – something which seemed almost inconceivable. But they were well informed.

Strahan was no ordinary convict settlement: it was designed for convicts who had committed a second crime and were in danger of becoming bushrangers. As Sorell, the Colony's Lieutenant Governor, and Strahan's founder, stated: it was to be a 'Place of Ultra Banishment and Punishment'. Robert Hughes puts it more plainly: for the ten years from its foundation in 1822, it was 'the worst spot in the English-speaking world'.

The convicts were lodged on Sarah Island, a small, bleak island in the middle of Macquarie harbour. After a scant breakfast, they rowed to shore and transported timber from dawn to dusk, often wading up to their necks in icy water, before rowing back to the island for a basic meal and sleep. In addition to the lumbering, they rowed up to twenty kilometres a day. Few survived more than a couple of years.

Even among these recalcitrant prisoners, there were those who were considered more ungovernable than others. These extreme cases, whom the authorities wished to separate from the other prisoners, were left each night on Grummet Island, a small exposed rock in the harbour, with only their clothes to protect them from the constant rain and bitter cold. Peculiarly, few convicts committed suicide in Strahan. Instead, they would often kill a fellow prisoner, knowing that their trial, and inevitable execution, would take place in Hobart. At least murder allowed them to escape the earthly hell of Strahan just once before their death.

Just as in Port Arthur, the authorities in Strahan made little effort to prevent escapes. To disappear into the bush, even with provisions, was considered suicidal, and in the few recorded attempts, most escapees died. The only man to attempt escapes twice – and survive – was the celebrated Alexander Pearce, a convict from County Monaghan. His survival on both occasions was considered suspicious. Only after his second recapture did he confirm his means of survival: he had cannibalised his fellow escapees. That was more than enough to condemn him, and he died on the gallows.

At the time of my visit, Tasmania was still the only state in Australia where male homosexuality was a crime; it was only decriminalised the following year, in 1997. This ingrained homophobia is partly a legacy of the convict period. The merchant middle class, who had most to gain by the cessation of convict transportation – it would remove a stain from the island, draw more free settlers with skills to Tasmania, and encourage trade – used homosexuality in their argument for the end of transportation. They claimed that the enforced confinement in such enclosed quarters of such depraved men only encouraged the practice of sodomy – a word so horrific that it was often denoted in official documents simply by four asterisks. They won the day, and transportation to Tasmania ended soon afterwards, in 1853, following four decades of horror.

Leaving the town museum about an hour before dusk, I drove through the soft countryside and stopped at a deserted spot to look out over the harbour and its narrow entranceway, which the convicts tellingly called 'Hell's Gates'. The countryside around Strahan is strikingly like the west of Ireland, and as the light faded, beautiful shadows and tones spread over the vast harbour.

Swans serenely floated across the placid waters against a Cinemascope backdrop of bulrushes, small islets and distant blue mountains. For an instant, I felt as if I'd been transported to the shores of the Shannon or the Connacht lakes, and some of the Yeats verses I'd just been reading began to ripple inside me. The brutal contrast between the crushing events that had taken place here and the ethereal beauty of this lovely, lonely place reduced me to a state of sorrowful wonder. Suddenly I felt as gut-scraping a hankering for Ireland as I've ever had.

As I gazed out over this idyllic scene, a story I'd read about one of the last Tasmanian Aborigines came into my mind. Lying near death from stomach sickness on Flinders Island, she looked out towards the nearby mountains and the coastline of Tasmania, still visible through the cabin window. Weakly raising herself up from her bed, she gestured yearningly towards the nearby island and gasped 'That my country!' Then, falling back heavily onto the bed, she died shortly afterwards.

Feeling saturated with loneliness, I soon left the harbourside and drove back along the gravel road to my empty hostel. On my own in the large common room, I watched some television in silence while my dinner cooked. An hour later – my unfinished plate still in front of me – I got up from the table and walked over to the hostel payphone and did what no early inhabitant or convict of Van Diemen's Land ever could. I picked up the receiver, dialled a number, and listened quietly as the voices of my family talked to me lovingly from a world away.

Up the Queensland Coast

East Coast
New South Wales & Queensland

N

York Peninsula

Cape Tribulation

25

unsealed road

24

Cairns

22

Magnetic Island

20

19

NORTHERN

17

Whitsunday Islands

QUEENSLAND

Mackay

out of petrol

Rockhampton

TROPIC OF CAPRICORN

Bundaberg

Fraser Island

12

SOUTHERN

11

10

QUEENSLAND

9

Brisbane

7

6

5

Coffs Harbour

tyre blow-out

NEW SOUTH

Port Macquarie

WALES

Newcastle

Sydney

PACIFIC

OCEAN

1. Sydney
2. Newcastle
3. Port Macquaire
4. Coffs Harbour
5. Byron Bay
6. Nimbin
7. Surfers Paradise
8. Brisbane
9. Noosa
10. Gympie
11. Rainbow Beach
12. Hervey Bay
13. Fraser Island
14. Bundaberg
15. Rockhampton
16. Mackay
17. Airlie Beach
18. Whitsunday Islands
19. Bowen
20. Townsville
21. Magnetic Island
22. Mission Beach
23. Cairns
24. Port Douglas
25. Daintree
26. Cape Tribulation

Big Bertha

After a year in Sydney, names from the backpacker journey up the east coast, such as Byron Bay, Fraser Island, the Whitsundays and Cairns, had taken on almost magical properties for me. Just when would I finally get to see them for myself?

This nagging question was obviously playing on my mind, as after my return from Tasmania I kept having the same dream. In it I'd travelled to the north-eastern corner of Australia, to the very tip of the dog's ear of the continent, and felt like I'd fallen off the edge of the world. It was as if I'd finally reached a utopian land of endless sunbeams, virgin wilderness and days of bliss.

One August morning, waking up again from this recurring dream, my stomach full of butterflies, I knew it was time to go.

Finances – or specifically the need to pay off a bank loan and put further money aside – had delayed my departure to Queensland for over a year. But filing my annual taxes, I was mistakenly classified as a full resident and unexpectedly received a four-thousand-dollar rebate. Together with the five thousand dollar I'd already saved, I was now quite flush, and my preparations began.

I initially thought that I'd buy a Greyhound or McCaffery bus ticket to Cairns. But when I told Scottish Andy about my tax windfall, his response stopped me in my tracks.

'So what type of car ya gonna buy?' he asked, matter-of-factly. 'Those McCaffery buses can be a real pain in the arse; you can get stuck beside some real bores, and they don't always travel to the more isolated places. But in a car you're your own man. You can share petrol costs. And it's a good way of meeting people too. It's a no-brainer.'

Andy was just back from a six-month, four-wheel-drive journey around the continent, so he was a man worth listening to. After the wonders of his travels, he couldn't disguise the fact that being stuck back in an office was almost killing him, or that as soon as he had enough money together again, he'd be off.

'Christ, four thousand bucks!' he muttered enviously. 'You lucky bastard! What I wouldn't give to be going with you!' As I walked back to my desk, his face glazed over, and he seemed to drift off somewhere far, far away from our city office. When I looked across at him five minutes later, he was still staring into space.

I suddenly couldn't wait to get started.

'Come round to ours, I've found just what you need,' Rob assured me over the phone that weekend.

When I'd explained things to him earlier that week, I knew he wouldn't let me down. But turning the corner onto his narrow street later that afternoon, I reckoned he must have finally lost his touch, if not his marbles.

Parked in front of his house was an enormous, decrepit-looking station wagon. Plonked on that tiny street, it looked as big as a juggernaut, and about as manoeuvrable as a beached whale.

'Rob, you *are* joking me?' I asked, as we stood side by side staring at the monstrosity. 'You don't really expect me to drive that thing, do you?!'.

'Nineteen seventy-eight Ford Falcon, four-cylinder, two-litre engine,' Rob replied with the assurance of a used-car salesman. 'Just what you want, mate.'

'But, Rob, I'll kill people,' I said in disbelief. 'Worse still, I'll kill myself.'

'Course ya won't,' Rob said, throwing me the keys as he jumped into the passenger seat. 'C'mon. Let's give her a spin.'

Minutes later, lumbering precariously through the narrow streets of King's Cross and Paddington, Rob chatted merrily away, ignoring my frantic efforts not to mount the kerb and mow down pedestrians recklessly walking along the pavement.

'Perfect, isn't she?' Rob said with a grin, while my sweaty palms slid down the steering wheel as, jerkily, I strained to keep the car on the road. 'And see these seats,' he said, pointing into the back. 'They go right down. Chuck those folded mattresses down on the floor and you can kip in the back. Save you on hostels. The last lad who owned this car even made up some nice blue curtains. Lovely, aren't they? So it doesn't get too bright in the morning, and you won't have any nosey bastards peeking in when you're at it in the back with some bird. What more could you want?'

Docked safely again outside the house, I leaned against a wall to steady my nerves while Rob sifted through the debris in the back of the car. There he found a battered water container, a spare fuel can, jump leads and various pots and pans; all of which would be very useful on the road.

'Just one last thing,' Rob added casually. 'Well two, actually. Sometimes if you drive it longer than a few miles at a time, a little smoke comes out from under the bonnet. But not to worry, I'm sure it just needs a good service.'

Paying no heed to my raised eyebrows, he continued. 'Oh yeah, the doors don't work properly, so don't lock them. Otherwise you'll have to climb in through the boot. That lock works fine.' There was nothing in this for Rob except a few beers, but backpacker pride urged him on. 'We ought to be able to get it for about one thousand two hundred bucks. The guy who owns it paid a grand and a half, but he's not the brightest, so we should be able to get him down a bit. Wadda ya reckon?'

'She's a beaut, mate,' the mechanic assured us when we collected her after her service. 'Cairns, you say? Sure, should get ya there if you treat her right. These old Ford Falcons last forever.' With this assurance I was ready to complete the transaction. One thousand one hundred dollars were handed over and, on account of her size, the car soon became known as Big Bertha, or just Bertha. I was almost ready.

Chris, the first person to respond to the car-share ads I placed around the city, was a six foot eight Philadelphian who told me he wanted to go scuba diving off the Great Barrier Reef in Cairns. 'Being a goddamn Seppo (Australian slang for 'Yank', from 'Septic Tank'), we guys don't get a visa here like you bums,' he explained to me when I picked him up in Coogee. 'So I've been working illegally as a house painter for the last six months. But hey man, I pump every dollar right back into the local economy. Ask any of the guys in the bar over there,' he added, nodding ruefully towards the Coogee Bay Hotel.

I picked up my two other passengers in King's Cross. Jelle (pronounced 'Yella') was a diminutive Dutch eighteen-year-old who had learnt his English, together with an astonishing range of American slang, from music videos and original-version foreign TV programmes and films in Holland. With fair hair and a gap between his teeth, he brimmed with energy and turned out to be a great travelling companion. Nili, on the other hand, was quick to let us know that after spending the last two years saving for this trip back home in Israel, she was determined to get full value for every cent.

But that was for the future, and as we drove north over the harbour bridge in sparkling sunshine, life seemed just fine. Yelle snapped a Doors cassette into the radio and sang along loudly in a tone-perfect American accent. *'Keep your eyes on the road and your hands up-on the wh-eee-el.'*

The Opera House fell away to our right through the bridge's heavy girders, and I had to pinch myself to think that I was finally on my way to Queensland and that nothing but open road and months of freedom now lay before me.

North to Brisbane

We took three days, travelling slowly through northern New South Wales, to reach Byron Bay, which is the first real place of interest along the coast.

At our first stop, in Port Macquarie, Nili complained that the petrol cost five cents more per litre than in Sydney. When Chris suggested we return to Sydney to fill up, Nili chose to ignore him and proposed instead that we visit Australia's only koala hospital, which happened to be in town. After ten minutes looking through wire mesh at a few bandaged bears chewing impassively on eucalyptus leaves, the party agreed to move on.

Coming into Coff's Harbour on our second night, we heard a loud 'plop' near the back axle and Bertha suddenly began to weave wildly along the road. Knowing immediately that we'd had a blowout, I held tightly to the steering wheel and managed to bring the car to a halt on the roadside.

When we finally shifted the mountain of gear from the back and lifted up the board to get at the spare wheel, we let out a collective groan. Underneath the board, there certainly were the *makings* of a wheel; unfortunately, neither the threadbare tyre, the airless black tube or the metal hub were attached to each other.

Although I was never to pay sufficient attention to car maintenance on my travels, that afternoon taught me about the need for good-quality tyres on Australia's highways. Anything threadbare or low-standard simply melted on the unmercifully hot, bitumen roads and soon peeled off the wheel like a snake shedding its old skin.

Showing great forbearance, no one asked the obvious question as to why I hadn't checked the spare wheel before buying the car. Instead Chris, the can-do American, calmly remarked that there had to be a mechanic somewhere in town. Sticking out his thumb to hitch (mobile phones were then still few and far between), he added wryly: 'Just as well we're so near civilisation.' We knew exactly what he meant as for the several hundred kilometres since leaving Sydney all we'd seen were the occasional small town or isolated servo (service station).

By chance, the driver who picked us up told us that there was a wrecker's yard about a kilometre away. When we entered the vast warehouse, I almost had an attack of vertigo. Wheels, exhausts, engines, and piles of sundry car parts rose up along the two-storey-high walls to the ceiling, and the wrecker foreman had little trouble in digging out a spare Ford Falcon wheel.

Only when we tried to change the wheel did we discover that our jack bent like plastic under the enormous weight of the car and our luggage. The mechanic who'd driven us back to Bertha then did another run to the warehouse and, coming back, changed the wheel himself with a heavy-duty jack. Then, showing the genuine decency I was to encounter everywhere on my travels, he gave us the jack in exchange for a token few dollars.

Byron Bay is the most easterly point in Australia, and its beaches are reputed to have the best surfing on the East Coast. But its famous hippie feel originates from the 'Aquarius Festival' which took place seventy kilometres inland in Nimbin in 1973. Inspired by events in California and espousing the 'love not war' ideals of the 1960s, the festival attracted young people from the cities, and ever since, Byron has been the hippie Mecca of Australia.

The town continues to have a palpable fun and energetic feel to it. Walking down the long main street the following day, we were greeted cordially by passing middle-aged hippies going about their business. In the banks, shops and bars, people were friendly, unpretentious and genuinely free-spirited, offering us a foretaste of the easy, open-air lifestyle that awaited us further north in Queensland.

After a few days lazing around town, we set out one afternoon into the creamy, dreamy hills above Byron and soon came to Bangalow's hippie market. The place was awash with tarot readers, hemp shirts, vegetarian stalls, psychedelic illuminated clocks, hippie jewellery, wood furniture, and of course the sweet smell of marijuana. At the hair-wrap stands, hunkered-down girls were getting their hair coloured with threads and laces. A guy who did hair wraps on Noosa beach later told me that he often brought in more than fifteen hundred bucks a week. As this was tax-free, it allowed him a nice beach lifestyle, he said, and to drive a Mercedes. After that, the seemingly ubiquitous hair-wrap stands in Queensland made a lot more sense.

Bangalow might have been an oasis of the Aquarian lifestyle, but later that afternoon we discovered that Nimbin clearly was not. It was just seedy. Drugs abounded; opening the car door, an over-weight, unshaven man in his mid-thirties cycled up to us on a child's BMX bike. Trying not to knock his knees against the handlebars, he whispered out from the side of his mouth: 'Hey man, want any butts?' He clearly wasn't in the Pablo Escobar league.

The hippie museum, with its psychedelic displays and intriguing hand-written notes from foreign visitors, was worth the visit, but the rest of town seemed very rundown. Either strung-out or stoned, adults well past experimental college age hung out in the few cafés or on the street ignoring their grimy, wild-eyed kids, who trailed after them like street urchins. Graffiti in the public toilets and on the street walls talked about dealers who'd been shot by the fascist police and other aggravations of this unjust society. Nimbin seemed to have lost something along the way since 1973, and I was glad to leave it later that afternoon to return to Byron.

Enjoying the vast beach by day and partying in the hostel bar by night, the two days we'd intended to stay soon turned into a week. By then I decided that if I was ever to get to Cairns, it was time to push on. But cracks had formed in our travelling party and I genuinely wondered if I would now be travelling on alone.

Nili, on her Spartan budget, had already moved into a hostel outside town which cost a dollar less a night, and also threw in a free toast-and-coffee break-fast. Chris, adopting a contrasting money management style, seemed to have travelled the eight hundred kilometres to Byron only to continue his party ways from the Coogee Bay Hotel. But not only was he almost broke, he also fancied his chances with a cute Melbourne girl we'd met in the hostel.

I hadn't the heart to tell him that he was wasting his time; Jelle had already clicked with her two nights before, and both he and the girl seemed completely smitten. Seeing this, I expected Jelle to say he'd be staying behind as well. But after a bit of heart-wrenching, he decided to 'keep his eyes on the road', as his Doors heroes suggested. So the following morning we said our goodbyes to Chris and, just past the nearby town of Tweed Heads, we crossed the state border into Queensland.

A week in Byron had accustomed us to the sunshine, vast beaches and back-to-nature living which we were quickly to learn are typical of Queensland. So it was ironic that we spent our first night in the 'Sunshine State' (as Queensland car registration plates vaunt) in the concrete resort of Surfers' Paradise. 'Surfers' lies at the heart of the glitzy strip of high-rise hotels and loud nightclubs of the Gold Coast. Being Australia's Ibiza, it is mobbed with 'ockers', Australia's version of yobs.

We hated the place. After a big night out in one of the town's many nightclubs, we left the following morning and an hour later arrived in Brisbane, the state capital.

Southern Queensland

Torrential rain beat down on the tin roof of the Banana Benders Backpackers Hostel as we checked in later that morning – a clear sign that we were now approaching the tropics. Still trying to find our feet after the good times in Byron, and weighed down by our hangovers from Surfers, we began to unpack lethargically in the dorm room. But someone soon walked in behind us whistling chirpily and, happy for the distraction, we introduced ourselves.

Drew was a brawny, unkempt forty-year-old, and as he oddly proffered his left hand for me to shake, I looked down with curiosity to see why. It was then that I saw that his right hand was swaddled in white bandages so thick that it seemed as if he had just stepped out of a Tom and Jerry cartoon. After a few minutes of small talk, despite the subject so obviously hanging in the air, he still hadn't explained; so I asked the question.

'That. Ah yeah,' he grinned, looking down at his injured hand as if he'd only just noticed it. 'Crack-up, isn't it?' And by way of explanation, he began telling us about himself.

'I'm a gold miner, yeah. Work in a place in the interior, few hundred Ks east of here. Pretty handy money, I reckon. Pull in about three thousand bucks a week. I've been in the game for fifteen years, mate. I'll be getting out though soon enough, I reckon, maybe in about two years. Should have enough to retire on then, buy a boat and a place by the ocean. Could make a good living bringing tourists out on fishing trips. Those folk spend a packet. Think about it, guys,' he said with a satisfied grin, 'sitting there with a rod in the water, feet up on the back rail, cold tinny in your hand, watching the sun go down over the ocean. Now that's the life, don't ya reckon?'

But he still hadn't explained his mummified hand. So I obliged with another prompt.

'Ah yeah, that. Got my finger blown off, didn't I. Silly bugger, eh?' he said, throwing his eyes up to heaven as if to make light of it. 'They stitched it back on though, and I ought to get some compo. 'Bout 20k this time I reckon, which ain't bad.'

But even with his restored finger, I noticed, he was still one short. 'Ah yeah, see all the fingers on me right hand been blown off at some time or other, and all except one have been sown back on. But mustn't grumble, four's better than none, eh?' But I wasn't convinced, as with his thumb the size of a scrawny finger jutting out lopsided from underneath the bandages, his hand looked a complete mess.

But he was clearly enjoying the attention and was far from finished. Leaning down very deliberately, he picked a red handkerchief up from the floor and stuffed it carefully into the breast pocket of his cheap suit resting on a wire hanger at the end of the bunk beds. Then, slowly dusting it down, he waited for me to take the bait.

'Looks very dapper,' I remarked laconically.

'Gotta look nice for my big day tomorrow, don't I mate?' he continued, with forced bonhomie. 'Off to court in the morning. That's why I'm up in Brizzy. Up on a few charges, ya see. Drunk and disorderly, damage to property and, oh yeah, assault and battery.'

Eight miners including himself, he explained, had got into a pub fight and smashed the place up quite badly. That accounted for the first two sets of charges. The bar owner had stepped in and got his leg broken, explaining the assault and battery.

Drew smiled happily. 'It was a blast, mate. I'd do it again tomorrow. What else is there to do in a small mining town if you're up for a bit of fun?'

He seemed blasé about the outcome of the trial. He reckoned he'd either get a few-thousand-dollar fine to compensate the bar owner or a few weeks in the slammer. He seemed to prefer jail.

'With this busted finger I'm on full pay. Might as well be sitting on my arse in jail while it heals instead of shelling out a few thousand bucks on a bloody fine, eh?'

An hour later, Jelle tracked me down in the common room. 'Drew wants to go for a bag of chips and a beer, you wanna come?'

Down in the chipper, we soon saw that Drew wasn't quite the man of means he'd let on to be. Perhaps we shouldn't have been surprised – earlier he'd told us he'd originally gone to the mines to sell drugs before realising he could earn more working the pits. He only needed a dollar loan to cover his food. But despite being skint, he still suggested we go for a few beers. He was having cashflow problems, he explained with a laugh and a wink as the first round arrived, and I paid. 'The ex-wife's sucking me dry for alimony, and the kids, ya know . . . ?' he added, as Jelle forked out for the second round. When we got to the third round I decided it was time to go. Drew called me a wowser – Australian for 'dry-shite' – but by then Jelle had formed the same opinion as I had.

We slept that night with our valuables under our pillows. Luckily, the next morning they were still there, and Drew was gone.

Like most Queensland towns, Brisbane is bright, laid back and friendly. But strolling around that day what I most remember was not the physical town – which was mostly uninteresting – but the moment Jelle turned to me and, with searching eyes, asked me did I believe in God?

Seeing me taken aback by the abruptness of his question, he tried to explain. His father, he said, had been blind, and so growing up he would always be asking Jelle questions. From the warmth in his voice I could tell they had been very close. They'd chat for hours at a time, and Jelle grew up recreating the world he saw all around him. He would describe a landscape, or a person's appearance, or the sense he had when he saw the colour red or turquoise, or what a foreign country looked like on television. But not long before, his father had suffered a long, difficult death from leukaemia. And Jelle had had to watch it all, without describing it to anyone but himself, for over a year.

When his father finally died, he was utterly lost. Why did his father have to go through such a horrible, painful death, and where was he now, he asked. Virtually locking himself into his room for six months, in a rage he mulled it over incessantly and thought he was 'going nuts'. And that's why he'd left Holland, alone, at the age of eighteen. Still deeply grieving, he had to get away and find somewhere where he could figure out what the whole thing meant. And Australia seemed the right place to do it.

Noosa seemed to have a strangely European air to it when we arrived in the next morning. In contrast to Surfers and the Gold Coast, the Sunshine Coast north of Brisbane was obviously an upmarket holiday resort. The fact that the rain had stopped helped too: for the rest of my journey up the coast, I was to have almost unbroken sunshine.

It was here that Jelle finally left me. Ever since Byron, he hadn't been his usual bubbly self. He was love-struck and miserable, and just couldn't seem to get the pretty Melbourne girl out of his head. So it was no surprise when that evening he returned very sheepishly to the hostel and spurted out: 'I've just bought a one-way ticket back to Byron, the bus is leaving tomorrow morning. I'm really sorry but . . . .'

There I stopped him, told him to tell that Yank to get his ass up to Cairns, and we'll all go diving on the reef together in a few weeks. For the first time in a few days, a familiar grin lit up his face, and after a few beers together we parted that evening in great spirits.

Seeing him off on the bus the next morning left me free to spend a few hours on my own the following day. Enjoying my time alone, I wandered through the coastal national park, spotting wild koalas, and swimming in the small ocean inlets.

That evening, for the first time since leaving Sydney a fortnight before, I gave my liver a night off and went to bed early with a book. Absorbed in the read, I hardly noticed as someone came into the empty dorm and began rustling through a plastic bag in their rucksack.

'Sorry mate, hope I'm not disturbing you?' a thick Australian accent whispered to me. Looking up, I saw a fair-haired, bearded man in his mid-forties. 'No worries,' I replied, but instead of returning to the book, we began talking. And over the next hour, as is often the case when travellers meet, he recounted more to me about himself than perhaps he had told anyone in years.

He'd only divorced two years before, he said. 'So now I'm doing what I should have done when I was your age – see some of this bloody great country.' He'd left Scotland for Australia twenty years before, just after he got married.

'There was nothing doing in Britain at that time. I was twenty-three, she was nineteen. So we decided to emigrate. Either Canada or Australia, we reckoned. We saw both on the telly. Canada looked bloody cold, Australia seemed hot. And that was what decided it for us.' He let out a deep, mellow chuckle at the memory of it. 'Came down on one of the last assisted passages. Nineteen seventy-three it was. Only cost us a tenner. Not bad, eh? What would you get for a tenner nowadays?'

The first time he went back to his mother, and his old home, was seventeen years later. He returned to the old pubs and hangouts, half expecting to see his old friends still there. But everything and everyone seemed to have changed or moved on. 'I've mostly good memories of it all, ya know! But it made me realise that Australia was home now. Can't ever see myself going back now.'

Envying the ease with which you could get into Australia just a quarter of a century before, I wished him good night and soon drifted off to sleep.

Perhaps his story had played on my imagination overnight, as the next morning I decided on a whim to get off the backpacker trail and head off somewhere quiet for a few days on my own. Glancing at the map, a place-name caught my fancy. So stocking up with enough food for a few days, I wove through dreamy pale hills and sleepy clusters of houses beyond the town of Gympie, and reached the small seaside hamlet of Rainbow Beach.

Rainbow Beach

Driving into Rainbow Beach, I thought I'd arrived into 'Summer Bay', the small fictional town in the Australian soap *Home and Away*. Rainbow Beach had one shop, a petrol station, a surf club, a caravan park and a bar. But soon learning that it had no hostel, I got directions to a small guesthouse about a kilometre up from the beach, and checked in.

As I was writing up my diary that evening, my pasta bubbling behind me, a middle-aged woman came into the kitchen. 'All right if I boil some water? Could murder a coffee.' Chatting as she put on the kettle, I listened to her story, which uncannily echoed the one I'd heard only the night before.

'There I was only a few months ago in the city waiting on my divorce to come through,' she explained, 'and I thought, to hell with it, what am I doing here? I'm a free woman now. I can do whatever I bloody well want. So I thought "let's travel", always wanted to see more of this country.' She'd come to Rainbow Beach intending to stay for only two days. But then her car had broken down.

'The mechanic told me it'd take a few days for the parts to arrive, but when it was fixed, I stayed. Been here almost two weeks now – kinda like it here. Reckon I'll know when it feels like the right time to move on.'

Like most Australians, she had seen very little of the continent before, and the country struck her as a revelation. 'Have you been down to the beach yet?' she asked in amazement. 'It's stunning! All those colours. That's why it's called Rainbow Beach, ya know. They say there are fifty-three different colours of sand all along the beach. It goes on forever too. If you've a four-wheel drive, they reckon you can drive all the way along the beach to Noosa – and that's about ninety Ks. There's an Aborigine Dreamtime about it too,' she added, as she grabbed her hot water from the kettle. 'About the colours, I mean. You can read about it on a plaque thingy down by the beach.'

A Dreaming, or Dreamtime, is associated with almost every significant physical feature in Australia. In *Songlines*, Bruce Chatwin describes them as 'Aboriginal Creation myths [that] tell of the legendary totemic beings who had wandered over the continent in the Dreamtime, singing out the name of everything that crossed their path – birds, animals, plants, rocks, waterholes – and so singing the world into existence'. It didn't take me long to find the plaque explaining Rainbow Beach's Dreamtime the following morning down along the long seafront.

In the Dreamtime, it recounted, a beautiful woman was snatched from her people by a very cruel man, who brought her to what is now Rainbow Beach. He left her to go hunting every day, and in her misery she would sit on the sands and gaze up at the sky. Over time, she fell passionately in love with the rainbow. One day, when the wicked man was away hunting, she decided to escape. But as she was fleeing down the beach, the man suddenly returned and, seeing her running away, threw his giant boomerang at her. But this was no ordinary boomerang: it contained within it all the evil of the world.

Seeing the boomerang, she fell down on her knees in terror and pleaded with her beloved rainbow to save her. Looking up, she saw that the rainbow had placed itself in the way of the evil boomerang to protect her. When the gigantic boomerang smashed into it, the rainbow shattered into a million pieces and showered its fragments onto the shore below. And they are still visible there today in the iridescent sands of Rainbow Beach.

Perhaps this Dreamtime charmed me more than I knew, because for the next three days I seemed to do little except wander alone along the beach or drift up into the iridescent sand-dunes and lie there for hours reading, or just looking out at the sea and sky.

What, I was beginning to wonder, was I really doing here? All I seemed to have done since I'd arrived in Australia was drink beer and read books. I knew, sure, that I'd wanted to get away from Dublin for some time, but still, why here? Why Australia?

A few months before, reading David Malouf's *The Conversations at Curlew Creek*, I was reassured that I wasn't alone in the powerful response I felt to the peculiar light and soaring skies of this continent. In this novel, he uses the character of a nineteenth-century Irish character to describe the experience. 'Some quality of the country, some effect of the high clear skies, so unlike the skies of Ireland, drew you on into an opening in yourself in which the questions that posed themselves had no easy sociable answers, concerned only yourself and what there was at last, or might be, between you and the harsh, unchanged and unchanging earth, and above, the unchanged, unchanging stars.'

Since crossing into Queensland, the limitless, impassive sky of this country had begun to affect me too. In such pristine freshness, so uncluttered by overbearing historical figures or physical vestiges of 'civilisation', Australia is a place where your mind can roam widely in utter freedom. Perhaps D. H. Lawrence had got it right. 'You feel free in Australia,' he wrote. 'There is a great relief in the atmosphere, a relief from tension, from pressure. An absence of control or will or form. The sky is open above you, and the air is around you. Not the old closing-in of Europe.'

And it was thoughts of that 'old closing-in' that came back to me in Rainbow Beach. What I was doing here in Australia on a second temporary visa I couldn't answer. The reasons were too vague. Things just seemed open and fresh here, and most of the time it felt good.

Somehow, though, I still felt uneasy, and at odds with the things around me. Besides having at some stage to get a proper job – something difficult to do on a temporary visa – it was unlikely that, long term, I'd be able to stay in Australia. And then where would all this reading and wandering get me? Was there something tangible I could ever get from it? I still had a sense that there was some purpose to my travelling, but maybe I was just kidding myself and only wasting my time?

Finding myself all het up after these ruminations, I'd then set off walking down the miles of beach, and half an hour later I could hardly recall what had so riled me. Something about this place had seeped into me and had soothed me deeply.

After a few days on my own, I decided I needed some company. Swinging open the doors of the sole bar in town, I was confronted by twenty red-faced men gathered in loud and very drunken groups around the bar. They all had crew-cuts and were wearing identical black T-shirts, as if they were part of some sort of club or association.

One drunk, quite the worse for wear, thumped the Red Indian in full feathered headgear on his T-shirt, almost sending himself toppling over. 'See this shirt, mate?' he belched to his slightly less inebriated friends, as he steadied himself against a table. 'See this shirt? This ain't coming off for eight days. I gotta sleep in it, swim in it, shower in it, bloody shit in it! See, because this ain't coming off, no, not for eight days!' This declaration was met by a storm of guffaws.

The scene was wild, but there was no other pub in town. So, steeling myself, I strolled up to the bar and ordered a VB. The service was slow, as a war council seemed to be taking place between the two barmen and some of the drinking club. A few minutes later, the barmen emerged from the back room with two large bottles of Bundaberg rum and a long-chord electric hair clippers. At the sight of them, the place immediately exploded with whoops, roars, and raucous Indian battle cries.

I asked a semi-sober patron beside me what was going on. Gruffly he explained that the drinkers were builders en route to Fraser for their summer shutdown holiday. (I later learnt that 'Indian Heads' is a place on Fraser Island.) They had dared the two barmen, in exchange for a bottle of rum and a T-shirt, to join them in shaving their heads. The builders, he said, only wanted scalps.

Two bar stools were placed just outside the door and everyone poured outside to watch and whoop on the show. One barman had long, surfie, sun-bleached hair, but no mercy was shown, as every strand of it was soon shorn off by the electric razor. The scalping over, each barman was presented with a black T-shirt and a bottle of rum, as ceremoniously as if they'd just won a Formula 1 car race. Finishing my beer outside, I saw the surfie reappear and gather up into a plastic bag what had once been his long, thick locks of golden hair. I really hoped he liked rum.

Knocking back my beer, I walked slowly back up the hill to the guesthouse, feeling dreamy and utterly detached from the world and everything that had just happened down at the bar. The night was limpid and warm, and tilting my head back I looked up at a glorious night sky. Garbled voices floated up the hill from the bar, but there wasn't a soul around, and I felt as if I was on my own under this starry universe.

Still buzzing from the last three days, a phrase – or was it a line of poetry? – once again came ebbing and flowing at the very edge of my memory. Just before it slipped away, I finally managed to grab it. '*Ces espaces infinis . . .*' Yes, that was it! Pascal's Pensée. '*Le silence eternel des ces espaces infinis m'effraie*' ('The eternal silence of these infinite spaces terrifies me').

That's how I felt. *That's* what hadn't sat right with me for the last few days. Here, under the enormity of the natural universe, something had felt just not right. Something I couldn't 'get'. It intimidated me in Ireland, and it intimidated me all the more here under these massive, high skies. Was this part of something I was in Australia to do? To figure out why those yawning spaces in my mind and the world so unsettled me? Was it really that simple?

Or was I just overcomplicating things? Why was I not happy just getting drunk and soaking up the sun? That'd make life a heck of a lot simpler. But whatever it was, I wasn't going to resolve it in Rainbow Beach. So early the next morning, I packed up Bertha and set off towards Hervey Bay, the embarkation point for my next stop: Fraser Island.

Fraser Island

It was impossible to be inconspicuous travelling in Bertha. After been moored in so many hostel car parks, she was too big, too white and too odd-looking not to become well known to fellow backpackers. In turn, I was beginning to recognise the vehicles of other backpackers. So when I spotted a familiar blue Ford sedan as I pulled into the hostel in Hervey Bay, I knew I'd have good company for the evening.

It belonged to the two Swedes with whom Jelle and I had discussed the European experiment in Surfers one very long week before. 'But everything will rest on the Deutchmark! On the Germans!' one of them had lamented passionately. 'Now they will control everything! How can we let them? After they started two – not one, but *two*! – world wars!' Punctuating his remark with a wide sweep of his arm, he almost cleared the cluttered table of beer bottles.

A fourth Reich, however, seemed far from his mind when I found them minutes later sunning themselves by the hostel pool. It was good to be back to the sociability of a backpacker hostel, and that evening, over beers, I had no difficulty in arranging to join a group travelling to Fraser Island the very next day.

Fraser Island is one of the highlights of the journey up the Queensland coast. One hundred and twenty kilometres long, and up to twenty-two kilometres wide, it is the world's largest sand island, and boasts startling lakes, beaches, forests and myriads of bird species. Even how the island came to be named is itself the stuff of adventure stories.

It all began in 1836 when the *Stirling Castle* ran aground almost three hundred kilometres north of the island near present-day Rockhampton. The ship's captain, a Scot named Fraser, set out in the ship's pinnacle with his wife, Eliza, and the rest of the survivors in search of the settlement on Moreton Bay, modern-day Brisbane.

But only making it as far as what is now Fraser Island, they encountered an Aboriginal tribe named the Kabi. Captain Fraser was speared to death almost immediately. But being white and female, the Kabi believed Mrs Fraser to be *Mamba*, the spirit of a dead woman who had lost both her colour and her ability to talk their language while in the grave, and she was spared. She later claimed that in captivity she was forced to do brute work and survive on the scraps the tribe members threw away, and that she hid her wedding ring in the grass skirt she came to wear. It was this last claim that later gave Patrick White, the Australian Nobel Laureate, the title *A Fringe of Leaves* for his novel based on the story.

Her rescue was dramatic. John Graham, an escaped convict, had lived among the Kabi for several years, spoke their language and had a Kabi wife. Hearing that a white woman was now living among the tribe, and hoping for a pardon, he returned to Moreton Bay with the sensational news. He was subsequently despatched off again with a rescue party. But arriving back on Kabi tribal land there seemed little hope of rescuing Mrs Fraser without seriously endangering both her and the would-be rescuers.

And so Graham decided to walk boldly on his own into a camp of four hundred Kabi. After talking with the tribe for several hours, he eventually convinced them that Mrs Fraser was the lost spirit of his dead wife. Calmly the pair then left the camp and walked out together to the waiting white men.

Graham received a pardon, and the story was the talk of Australia; Mrs Fraser later wrote a book about her experience. Twenty years later, however, she was knocked down and killed by a tram in Melbourne. As Ned Kelly, another celebrated figure who also met his end in the same city, once observed acerbically: 'Such is life.'

The short ferry across to the island the next morning allowed me to get to know my group for the next three days. The seven of us came from six different countries: Norway, Korea, Germany, South Africa, Turkey and Ireland. Travelling with such eclectic nationalities was to become a feature of my Queensland trip; indeed, Bertha was to carry more than a dozen nationalities during this three-month journey.

Disembarking on the landward side, we set off in our rented four-wheel-drive over the rugged tree-lined roads across the island to the eastern shore. Although a few unsealed roads do exist, the one-hundred-and-twenty-kilometre-long beach skirting the ocean side of the island is Fraser's main highway. Rusty shipwrecks tilting in the shallow water litter the beach, and later we stopped at the *Maheno*, a former cruise liner and famous island skeleton, to clamber over its salt-eroded frame.

We joined another group just past Indian Heads that night to share dinner and stories around a blazing campfire. Emerging from the tent just after dawn, I saw one of the backpackers from the previous night, hunched up in his sleeping bag about a hundred metres down the beach, lost in solitary contemplation of the ocean panorama and the early-morning sun. Entranced by the sunrise he'd just witnessed, and – judging by the large camera at his side – also just photographed, he seemed oblivious to the danger of the dingo snaking up behind him.

Dingoes are commonplace on Fraser, and for the most part they are reasonably harmless. At worst they might nip at the legs of more timid backpackers when food is at hand. But this dingo wasn't looking for food. He must have seen the glinting camera by the backpacker's side, and was sidling up to grab it by its cloth strap. My warning shouts down the vast beach were drowned out by the roar of the ocean; by now the dingo was only metres away, and about to pounce. But just then the Buddha backpacker looked around, spotted the thieving dingo, sprang up and sent him scampering off.

He was lucky. No damage was done. Unfortunately over the next few years dingoes on Fraser became more brazen, and in 2001 they were to attack two young boys, killing one of them.

Dingoes were only the first of the many creatures I came to be wary of as I travelled further into Queensland. Very soon, I had to avoid ocean swimming altogether. Tiger sharks are known in these waters, and besides, it was almost box-jellyfish season. Box jellyfish are among the most lethal creatures alive; a sting from one causes a mini-paralysis that often results in a heart attack within seconds. As an antidote, most main beaches are equipped with bottles of vinegar: dosing the stung area with the mild acid can counteract the venom. The vinegar won't keep you out of hospital, but at least you might survive.

On our final morning on the island, in the bitter cold, I stumbled down from our camping area in a sheltered dune with my Norwegian and Turkish companions to watch the sunrise. Wrapped up in our sweaters and sleeping bags, rubbing ourselves to stay warm, we waited for the sun to appear. Strikingly, it soon did, shimmering slowly up over the ocean horizon.

In Ireland, dawn always seemed to act like a dimmer switch, slowly lighting up the day behind an opaque sky. But this was my first southern sunrise, and it was spectacular, the dazzle forcing us to shield our eyes from its full glare. The sudden heat on our bodies sent our senses tingling, and we returned up the beach for breakfast in high spirits.

Back in Hervey Bay that afternoon, freshly washed, we ate ravenously in the hostel bar. We were at last venturing into the delirious wonderment that the stunning sights of Queensland can induce. I drove off north again the next morning feeling as if I hadn't a care in the world.

Zucchini, chilli and avocado fields now began to line the road, as I was nearing Northern Queensland. Besides the changing scenery, I also began to notice the intensity of the sun; stepping out of the car, I could almost feel its rays bore into me. There is good reason why Queensland has one of the highest incidences of skin cancer in the world, and from then on I made sure to cover up well whenever I was out of doors.

With a current of balmy air cooling me through my driver's window, I sailed past the town of Bundaberg – home of Australia's most famous rum, made from the local sugar beet – and three hundred kilometres later, at Rockhampton, I crossed the Tropic of Capricorn and entered Northern Queensland.

Wanting to put more kilometres behind me before nightfall, I continued on northwards. However, less than an hour later the engine cut out. Using my momentum, I managed to free-wheel Bertha onto the scrub edge of the highway. I knew it was now too dark to do much, so collapsing the back seat, as Rob had shown me, I stretched out the deckchair mattresses and lay down for my first sleep in the car. Any repairs could wait until morning.

But I was soon jolted awake as a blinding light beam lit up the whole car. In my sleepy state, I thought I was having a close encounter of another kind, until I heard a booming roar crash past, rocking the car violently from side to side. Then I knew that a road-train – a vehicle the length of two articulated trucks – had just gone by. And they continued to hurtle thunderously past me all night. But I was dog tired, and despite the disturbance I slept well.

I woke up in an oven early the next morning but, quickly exiting, I was greeted by glorious sunshine. Life, I reckoned, could be worse.

Lifting the bonnet, I could see nothing obviously out of place. So I had little option but to get myself to a phone and call an NRMA (Australia's AA) mechanic to get things checked out.

Sticking out my thumb, a few cars passed. Then I saw a single container truck approach, thunder past and then suddenly slam on its airbrakes. It took more than a hundred metres to come to a halt, and I quickly ran after it. Hauling myself up into the high cabin, I was greeted by a man in his forties and his twelve-year-old son. They greeted my casually, but kindly. 'There's a servo 'bout twenty Ks up the road. Ought to be a phone there. That all right for you?'

Very grateful, I thanked them warmly but he shrugged it off. 'Ah, forget it. I'd like someone to do the same for me if I was stuck.' Then, bashfully, he turned to the boy: 'Anyway, you wouldn't mind a bite, would ya son? We can get breakfast there, eh?'

They were bringing a load from Sydney to their hometown of Mackay further up the coast. As we drove, he told me about the vehicle and life on the road; how every fill-up cost a few hundred dollars and how each time he overtook someone the truck used up several litres of petrol. I realised then that stopping for me had not only thrown him off his schedule but cost him fuel. When I later told Australians about this kind turn, they were astounded. Road trucks never stop for hitch-hikers, they said. Not ever! And I never tried to hitch from one again.

Twenty minutes later, I was on the phone to the NRMA, explaining to someone in a call centre in South Australia my exact location on this massive stretch of highway in Northern Queensland. 'Bruce Highway? Righto. About a hundred Ks north of Rocky? Someone will be there soon, OK?'

When the mechanic arrived, he only needed a few seconds under the bonnet to detect the problem. 'Run out of fuel, mate. Ya got a fuel can?' I felt a complete fool. He filled me up, charged me ten bucks for the petrol, started my engine and drove off. In consolation, I told myself that my fuel gauge was obviously broken, as it still read half-full. But I might have saved myself quite a bit of bother if I'd had it repaired in Mackay, the next town. But implacable traveller that I was, I drove on instead another eighty kilometres to Airlie Beach, the gateway to the Whitsunday.

The Whitsundays

The Whitsunday Islands are one of the many features Cook named on his famous voyage up the east coast of Australia in 1770. Other places include the Glasshouse Mountains (named after a range in his native Yorkshire), Double Point Bay (which he believed to be two islands), Magnetic Island (which he felt had thrown his ship's compass off course), and Dejection Bay (where he almost ran aground). The Whitsundays he named to mark the day they were sighted. But as he failed to take into account that he had crossed over the international date line, they were actually spotted on a Monday.

There are many misconceptions about Cook. He didn't discover Australia, as many people think – the Dutch had landed along the coast of Western Australia and Tasmania over a century before. On that famous voyage to Australia, he still had the rank of Lieutenant – the 'Captain' only came on his return to Britain. Nor was he the commander of the First Fleet of convicts and soldiers to arrive in 1788, as by that time he had already been dead for ten years.

But what is true is that Cook *was* an astonishing navigator. Not only did he rediscover the importance of fresh fruit to ward off scurvy, but he also charted vast areas of the southern oceans, which had great significance in the development of cartography and the expansion of the British Empire. After rising up through the ranks, he became famous in Britain not so much for his discoveries but for the journals which he published of his voyages. In them, the mettle and astute observations of this self-made Renaissance man shine through.

One famous passage about the Aborigines illustrates this: they 'may appear to some to be the most wretched people upon earth; but in reality they are far happier than we Europeans, being wholly unacquainted not only with the superfluous, but with the necessary conveniences so much sought after in Europe. . . . They live in a tranquillity . . . the earth and sea of their own accord furnishes them with all things necessary for life. . . . This, in my opinion, argues that they think themselves provided with all the necessaries of life, and they have no superfluities.'

It was perhaps fortunate that Cook's journals were such best-sellers, as they helped provide for his widow in her old age. Not only was her famous husband now dead, but of the thirteen children she had brought into the world, not one survived into adulthood, leaving the famous navigator no direct heirs.

The Whitsundays are thronged with visitors ranging from backpackers to luxury holidaymakers, undertaking scuba-diving courses or sailing trips, or just relaxing on some of the more upmarket holiday island resorts. If not arriving by air, most visitors access the islands through the tourist town of Airlie Beach.

The backpacker route north is a well-worn path, so it was no surprise, shortly after my arrival, to see a familiar figure walking perkily down the main street. Tim and I had crossed paths with uncanny frequency: in Port Maquarie, Coff's Harbour and Byron Bay. Together we had visited Castlemaine Brewery in Brisbane and dodged the dingoes on Fraser. We were to meet at almost every stop before Cairns, and subsequently to travel together to Uluru.

From Stratford-on-Avon, Tim had taken a year's break from his quantity-surveying job in London to travel the world. His affable and polite demeanour belied a mischievous sense of humour and a street-smart savvy. He had after all already travelled much of South America alone, and after Australia he was to venture through Asia before returning to England.

Besides having someone with whom to share a beer, I was looking forward to getting his take on the islands. I could see from his bloodshot eyes that he had been spending long hours scuba diving (he had in fact just finished a scuba-diving certificate) and that night he told me what he'd heard about the various sailing-tour companies around town. Acting on his recommendation, I booked a three-day trip around the islands on a twelve-berth yacht. We left two days later.

The group was the usual motley mix of nationalities: English, Canadian, Australian, German and myself. But one person immediately made an impression. Already middle-aged at thirty-four, Mark had spent a decade in the British army and now drove trucks for a living around the English Midlands.

I first bumped into him in the 'bottle shop' (Australian for 'off licence') in the marina. Between swimming and snorkelling, it looked as if we'd be having an active few days, so I suggested we go halves on a slab of twenty-four stubbies. Twelve beers, I reckoned, would be enough for each of us over two nights' drinking. 'Oh nooo! I don't think so,' Mark gasped, reacting in horror as if I'd just asked to sleep with his mother. Then, clutching his full slab of beers even closer to his chest, he quickly sidled away from me to the safety of the yacht.

Anchoring the first night off one of the islands, we ate under a canopy of stars as Mark made good headway on his slab of Castlemaine. Next morning, a glorious sky and sea animated everyone on board as we got ready for the full day ahead; all, that is, except Mark. His head emerged above deck, he took one squint at the bright sunshine, and he immediately returned below to his bunk. Badly hung over, the rocking of the boat upset him. So half an hour later, his deathly-pale face appeared on deck again. Putting on sun cream was an effort too far, and for much of the day Mark slept on deck. On the third day, he was forced below once more, this time lobster-red and suffering from sunstroke. He really should have shared that slab.

While Mark was going through his miseries, we were revelling in the beauties and activities of the Whitsundays. It is the most stunning place to visit on the east coast. The immaculate beaches, the crystal-blue seas, the sapphire skies – they were all impossibly perfect. Whitehaven Beach on Whitsunday Island itself, perhaps the most famous in Australia after Bondi and Cable Beach in Broome, is as white as snow. Each year, Craig the skipper told us, after a charity barbecue, dozens of volunteers scour its talcum sands for litter down to the size of a matchstick. And the beach we experienced the next morning was indeed pristine.

Despite all the talk about diving in Cairns, the Great Barrier reef actually stretches along most of northern Queensland. Starting at the coast off Bundaberg, a hundred kilometres south, the reef extends over two thousand kilometres northwards as far as Papua New Guinea. During our cruise, we had many stops to snorkel and glance down at the luminous fish floating calmly over the wondrous coral plants of the Great Barrier Reef. One day we hand-fed fish with chunks of bread as they swam tamely all around us.

The reef also seemed safe from sharks. At least the skipper, sitting safely at the wheel, pronounced that it was. And if he *did* spot any suspicious fins, he promised he'd give us a shout.

Coming out of the water, the skipper's mate would have ready a sumptuous meal of fish or meat followed by tropical fruit to satisfy our hungry appetites. Then, as we went off to play again, or sunbathe on the upper deck, she cheerfully cleaned up after us. We were treated like lords, and for three days we were allowed to forget that we were only lowly, skinflint backpackers. It was a delight.

After those few days of near-paradise, we didn't want the sense of fun and exhilaration to end. But people had to move on, and after a big night on shore we dispersed to continue our journeys; some northwards to Cairns, others returning down to Sydney. This was a side to backpacking I was still getting used to: in wondrous surroundings, making friendships quickly, talking youthfully and freely about everything under the sun, and then only days later saying goodbye, knowing it was unlikely that you would meet again.

But this time I didn't leave alone. Tay, the dark German from our cruise, wanted to drive with me to Townsville. He had a valid McCaffery's ticket to Cairns but he was fed up travelling by bus. At least by car, he reckoned, it would be more flexible, and he could see more of the landscape. With his aloof, seemingly arrogant manner, he didn't strike me as the most promising of travelling partners. But Townsville wasn't far, and his petrol money wouldn't hurt.

With such low expectations, therefore, it would have surprised me greatly as we set off the following morning to know that instead of sharing a day's journey, we would spend almost a month together travelling through some of the most famous places in Australia.

Magnetic Island

After over-indulging in the Whitsundays, it was a common practice for broke backpackers to pick up several weeks' work in the farmlands around Bowen, half an hour north of Airlie Beach. This provided enough funds for the final push up the coast and maybe even for another few weeks of partying in Cairns.

So approaching Bowan the next day, I wasn't too surprised when Tay suggested we check it out. A few weeks' work fitted in with his schedule and more cash, he reckoned, wouldn't go amiss in India, his next stop after Australia. But I didn't need the money and besides, I'd heard enough from an onion-nosed Irish survivor one evening in Airlie Beach to truly kill off all interest.

'It's good money,' he told me as he greedily slugged back a cold beer. 'But Christ, do they make you work. And do you know what gets most of the Irish and English backpackers? It's not so much the heat and the sun – which are brutal. It's salt! Yeah, you sweat like a pig in those fields, and unless you rake the salt onto your food – I usually ate loads of salt-crackers – you begin to feel a bit ill, and that's down to the amount of salt you're losing. But God, the heat is something else. Most lads come up thinking they're superman and trust me, they don't last long.'

He gave out a loud chuckle. 'These Irish lads I knew. Country boys. Strong as bullocks. Well used to hard, physical work. Started working one morning loading watermelons onto the truck. Gotta start just after dawn while it's still a little cool. Anyway, that sort of work is paid by weight, and these lads went at it like they were apples. By about eight they'd loaded so many they reckoned that a few weeks here they'd have made a fortune and were wondering just what all the fuss was about. Thought it was doddle.

'But then the sun really started biting and they gradually slowed down until by about half ten they were in tatters. Thought the melons were made of lead. They were destroyed. Reckoned no money was worth this, and fit to collapse they staggered back to the hostel. Left for Cairns the next day.'

He burst out laughing, obviously proud that he'd lasted the pace. 'Thought they were made of Kryptonite. Didn't even last till morning tea-break!'

But to make myself agreeable to my new travelling companion, I agreed to check it out. Not really sure what to expect, we pulled up outside a large building which we had been told was a farmhand hostel. Once inside the hallway, Tay and I watched in astonishment as bright-red zombies drifted in and out of doors, and up and down the sweltering corridor, in boxer shorts or bikini tops. When finally we got one of them to talk, he told us there wasn't much going on that day. 'It's Sunday. Nothing happens on Sundays. It's our only day off during the week, and everyone's either shattered from the week's work or horrifically hungover – usually both.'

He didn't seem to have an ounce of energy, and he talked with weary sarcasm. 'Not quite the Ritz, is it?' he asked, seeing us looking around at the grubby surroundings. 'Wouldn't be so bad though if you could maybe get some sleep. But in this heat? And God forbid there'd be air-conditioning. Sure what would you want that for in tropical Queensland, eh?' And as he disappeared down the furnace-like hallway, Tay and I looked at each other. It was time to go. We'd been standing inside for less than ten minutes and were already plastered in sweat: doing physical labour outdoors under this sun just didn't bear thinking about.

I soon came to admit that my initially poor impression of Tay was probably down to pure jealousy. Standing over six feet tall, with dark skin, eyes and hair, and a strikingly muscular physique, he could easily have passed for a male model. The girls on the Whitsunday cruise hadn't been slow to make this observation, as they lustily eyed up his figure on deck swishing around uninhibitedly in a sarong. Being an almost qualified doctor and speaking fluent English didn't hurt either.

And I was also wrong when I thought him a stereotypically arrogant German: his father was Lebanese – which explained his dark, Arabic features.

Although proud, he was not conceited, and soon proved to have a great sense of humour. We hit it off. So when he suggested in Townsville that we travel across to Magnetic Island together for a few days' R'n'R, I thought: 'Why not?'

Most of Magnetic Island is national park, with towering tree-covered mountains overlooking much of the coastal areas of this rugged, volcanic island. Mount Cook, at five hundred metres, is its tallest mountain and, naturally, Tay decided that this was the one we were going to climb.

The mountain terrain is so impenetrable, and the undercover so snake-infested, that to cut down on the number of forced searches required each year, the rangers hand out entrance permits to the area only very selectively. Tay went to the rangers' office that afternoon and was granted a two-person permit almost as soon as he'd opened the door. Astutely, he'd left me behind.

So it was only when he picked up a stout stick, as we set off from the base of the mountain just after dawn the next day, that Tay divulged the ranger's full instructions. We had to rustle the leaves and the ground before us, he told me. 'That way, the ranger said, the snakes will bite the sticks before they bite our legs.' Snakes are common in North Queensland and some, including the Taipan and the Brown snake, are among the most poisonous in the world. So thanking Tay for the information and allowing him to lead the way, we set off.

Being a medical student, Tay explained to me what to do if one of us was bitten. The cowboy movies always got it wrong, he said. Snipping the skin and 'sucking out the poison' only increases the blood flow, thereby speeding up the spread of the venom around the body. So if one of us was bitten, we agreed to leave a sweater and water with the victim and the other person would run for help.

But starting off, snakes didn't really seem to be the problem. Rather, the bush was so dense that after half an hour of climbing over and around and doubling back through logs, trees and overhanging branches and briars, and constantly testing the ground ahead of us for snakes, we'd find we'd only progressed about fifty metres and were invariably off-course.

Sweating, cut by brambles, cursing and most likely lost, we hacked our way through for another two hours without appearing to make any progress. We were getting nowhere, and were quite desperate. And by now we weren't even too sure of our way back. All we knew for certain was that we had to go up. Besides bringing us up the mountain – which was our objective after all – from a more elevated position we'd be able to get a better idea of our bearings, and what direction to take.

Just then we spotted a dried-up riverbed, which in wetter weather must run its craggy course down the mountain. It looked sheer and dangerous but it had two advantages: it was free from dense bush and it had somehow to lead *up* the mountain.

We moved quickly, moving upwards from rock to rock. Occasionally four-metre vertical rock faces blocked our way and we'd scale them nervously, knowing that a slip would send us scudding dangerously down the steep mountainside. An hour later, just as our legs were beginning to tremble from tiredness, we scrambled onto the top ledge of the mountain and reached the summit.

Elated at our achievement, but drained from the climb, we lay down on the ground to rest. Munching muesli bars and drinking water, we looked down at the green forest as it fell steeply down into the endless light blue of sky and ocean. How odd to be here, I thought. It was a midweek October morning. Most people I knew were now in an office somewhere, looking out at a cold grey sky, and here I was gazing down from a remote forested island into the blue Pacific. Sometimes I couldn't quite believe my luck in the life I was living.

But doing a lazy half-roll on the warm rock brought me a little down to earth. About a kilometre away, I saw another mountain peak towering about us and knew we couldn't have reached the top of Mount Cook, the island's tallest mountain after all. Tay followed my glance and let out a roar. Half-heartedly, he suggested we give the higher peak a go, but in colourful language I quickly put him straight on the idea.

We soon began retracing our steps downwards, which proved faster but much more hair-raising than the ascent. Safely down at the bottom of the river course, we still had to find our way out of the dense bush. Our map was now all but useless, so taking bearings from the sun, we began beating our way through dense forest. Finding another dry riverbed, we followed it for another kilometre and finally came out onto a dirt track, which soon led us to the joy of a small bitumen road. We now knew we were safe. Although we hadn't the least idea where we were, the island was so small that a bitumen road had at some point to lead us back to civilisation. And sure enough, it soon brought us to the main island road, from where we hitched a lift back to the tree-curtained entrance to our hostel.

That day's adventure gave me a new insight into just what the early explorers of Australia had undertaken.

For the last year in Sydney, I had swum at least five kilometres a week in Bondi or Glebe swimming pools, so I was fit, well-fed and strong. But even with a map and compass, we had become hopelessly lost after covering only a few kilometres of dense bush. And with only light backpacks to carry, we were still physical wrecks for about two days afterwards.

But the early explorers had travelled with heavy, rudimentary equipment, and a poor food and water supply into unknown terrain, which was at times almost inconceivably tortuous to traverse. Once on his crossing of the Blue Mountains in 1807 – being just one case in many – Blaxland and his seven men spent a whole day cutting through bush to travel just two kilometres. And after our failed attempt of Mount Cook, I never read another early-Australian-explorer story without feeling awe at those men's character and courage.

Leaving Magnetic Island, Tay decided to continue with me to Cairns, now only a few hours north. We stopped for two nights in Mission Beach, a former nineteenth-century Christian Missionary for Aborigines and now a delightful, tranquil haven. Of course I met Tim there, and together we went white-water rafting on the River Tully, a grade-four river, which has the highest rainfall on mainland Australia (only Strahan in Tasmania has higher).

And then, almost two months after leaving Sydney, I finally reached Cairns! And what a disappointment that turned out to be.

Cairns and Cape Tribulation

After hearing so much from returned backpackers in Sydney, I'd created a firm image of Cairns in my mind. It was an El Dorado; a free-spirited place where backpackers walked barefoot around the streets, each evening exchanging stories about their outback adventures, after yet another endless day scuba diving off the reef – which was surely only a hundred metres off yet another spectacular, golden beach.

But instead we arrived to wide mudflats where the stunning beach ought to have been. And rather than bumping into backpackers still in dreamy raptures after their lengthy travels, most of those we encountered had only whistle-stopped up the coast and were now in Cairns to booze in the sun.

Why hadn't they just gone to Ibiza, I thought. To have missed the wonderful isolation and natural beauty that gradually seeps into a person on the slow journey up the coast seemed to me a minor tragedy. When would a young person ever have the same chance again?

Perhaps this disappointment prompted us to leave town quickly and travel north to Cape Tribulation in the Daintree National Park at the entry to Cape York, the pointed dog's ear peninsula of Australia.

The day before, Tim had told us that the area around the Daintrees is one of the few places on earth where evolution has continued uninterrupted for the past 130 million years. In the 1980s there was a serious threat to the area by the powerful logging lobby, but the Hawke government – just as it had in Tasmania – declared the area a national park in 1988, and the ecosystem was preserved.

The Daintrees gave us our first taste of 'unsealed' – or dirt – roads. Driving carefully along the rutted roads, still unsure about Bertha's resilience, we saw a girl hitching. Despite the huge weight of our baggage and bodies – in addition to Tay and Tim, we were now carrying a fourth person named John – we pulled up. Shoving aside some gear, we wedged the girl's bulky swagbag in the back and she squeezed in beside Tim.

I'd never seen a real swagbag before, and I looked it over closely while stowing it in the back. Its base was padded and waterproof, like an insulated tent groundsheet. Otherwise it looked like a large sleeping bag with loose fastenings on its underside. In the morning, the girl later told us, she just threw her belongings inside, rolled it up, fastened it, and tossing it onto her back, was ready to hit the road again.

Cute and grungy-looking, the girl was in fact as hard as nails. She was the ship's cook on a fishing boat working out of Darwin.

'It's great,' she told us in her clipped Australian accent. 'It's a pretty small boat and we all muck in. I'm not just stuck cooking. Whenever they land a big catch I help the blokes out. Then it's all hands on deck. It's crazy work, twenty-hour days. Your hands get cut to ribbons with the fishing lines, the knives and the fish scales.' She proudly showed us her leathery and calloused hands as evidence.

She did two trips a year, each for three months; and on every return to Darwin she picked up a large pay cheque. 'There's no way to spend money on board except on cards and spliffs. And as I grow my own grass on the boat, almost all the money I earn goes straight into the bank.'

She'd already bought her piece of land – the yearning of every Australian – and still had enough money to go walkabouts for the other six months of the year. Hitching with her swagbag was cheap, and anyway she reckoned it was the best way to travel and meet people.

As she recounted her stories, we drove through winding, unsealed roads, past warning signs for saltwater crocodiles and crossing cassowaries (the shy, emu-like creatures who live in these rainforests), and finally arrived into one of the hostels of 'Cape Trib'.

An hour later, Castlemaine in hand (the only beer besides Toohey's sold at the bar), we found ourselves closely following the preparations for the evening's entertainment: a cane-toad race.

The organiser, like every other man in the bar, wore *Crocodile Dundee* shorts and singlet. Soon, clearing a few chairs and tables from the middle of the bar, he drew a large chalk circle about five metres in diameter on the floor and placed a large plastic dustbin upside down in the centre of the ring. His work done, he went off to the bar for a beer.

The stars soon appeared. Each was exceedingly ugly, with large, oily warts on their back and heads. But that didn't seem to deter the men, who held and stroked them affectionately like pet hamsters. A number was stuck onto each toad's back, and they were held up for view to the crowd gathering around the edge of the chalk circle. At auction, most toads went for ten or twenty dollars; those with the most colourful names went for as much as fifty. With prizes of two hundred, one hundred, and twenty dollars respectively for the first three winning toads, this race was clearly meant for fun and not for making fortunes.

The bidding over, the toads were dropped through a hole in the top of the bins, as the last money exchanged hands. Then, with a few sharps kicks and hollow thuds, the bins were lifted.

Dazzled by the sudden brightness and the towering giants screaming above them, most of the toads just sat stone still. A few, however, thought to escape this fearful din and hopped slowly towards the edge of the chalk circle. The winner was quickly scooped up by the nearest spectator, held up high and hailed as the champion.

To Tay's delight, 'Herman the German' won. Tim and John weren't too put out as 'The Whinging Pom' came third. And all three of them turned to me, highly amused, as 'The Laughing Leprechaun' hadn't even made it across the finishing line. Grinning from ear to ear as I pulled a long face, Tay threw his arm over my shoulders and turned me towards the bar. 'Come on, my little laughing leprechaun,' he chortled. 'This one's on me!' The contest might have only lasted seconds, but the after-race celebrations went on long into the night.

After almost two months of travelling, one day had long since drifted into another and standing at the hostel noticeboard the next morning, it took the four of us to figure out that it must now be November. Tim thought it might be Sunday, and Tay's watch said it was the eleventh of the month, so the poster about a local Sunday Remembrance Day fair had to be taking place that day. With nothing better to do, we decided to go along.

After weaving our way through a few kilometres of rainforest roads, we came to an odd collection of cars and four-wheel-drives parked outside two community buildings. After being made very welcome by the locals, we grabbed a few drinks at one of the tables and followed the others arriving at the event. As we turned the corner of the community buildings, we were confronted with one of the most impressive panoramas I was to see in Australia. At the end of an immense playing field, forested mountains soared upwards into an immense, sapphire sky; all afternoon my eyes kept turning back to it as if drawn by a magnet.

Not that there wasn't enough entertainment to amuse us, especially in the game of Aussie rules taking place. It seemed to involve about thirty men in various states of undress and of all ages, from their teens to their fifties, zipping around the gargantuan field. Although each of them carried a can or plastic cup of beer, as they raced along like whippets, plodded onwards like carthorses, leapt up for a high ball or barged into each other off the ball, not one of them spilt even the smallest drop. It was quite an art.

Towards late afternoon, a young man with a big bushy beard and strong face (reminiscent of the daguerreotype photograph of Ned Kelly taken just before his execution), stood up before the microphone and introduced locals to the stage to perform Australian songs and ballads. 'Look around you folks,' he cried out, pointing towards the forests and the enormous blue skies. 'Australia, Felix, the best bloody country in the world, and we're lucky bastards to be able to call it home.' Gazing at the glorious beauty around us, looking all the more magical towards sunset, it seemed that no truer word had ever been spoken. It really was 'God's country'.

We stopped in Port Douglas on our last night before returning to Cairns. Unable to spot any of the Hollywood cast filming *The Thin Red Line* in the local rainforest, we discussed our onwards travel plans. Tim told us that after flying from Cairns to Alice Springs, he had no idea how he'd travel the last, surprisingly long, five hundred kilometres to Uluru. A bus, maybe; he wasn't sure.

'What if you were to catch a lift?' I asked, looking him straight in the eye. He understood immediately. I suggested he get himself to Alice Springs and we'd take care of the details when we got there. Another wonderful journey beckoned.

The Outback:
Queensland Interior,
Northern Territories,
South Australia and Victoria

The Outback

Queensland Interior,
Northern Territory,
South Australia & Victoria

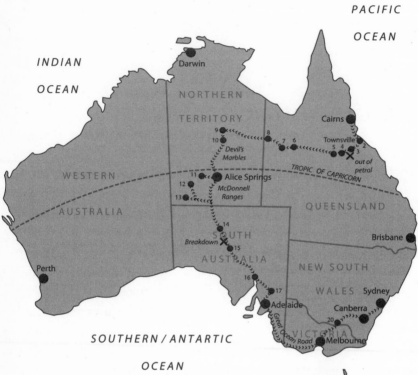

1. Cairns
2. Townsville
3. Charters Tower
4. Torrens Creek
5. Hughenden
6. Cloncurry

7. Mount Isa
8. Camooweal
9. Three Ways
10. Tennant Creek
11. Glen Helen
12. King's Canyon

13. Uluru
14. Cadney Homestead
15. Coober Pedy
16. Port Augusta
17. Barossa Valley
18. Adelaide

19. Melbourne
20. Wagga Wagga
21. Canberra
22. Sydney

0   1000kms

Into the Outback

By the time I got back to Cairns, I felt as rich in time as I'm ever likely to feel. With nothing apparently calling me back to the world, and with enough funds to allow me to travel for at least another six months, it seemed that I could keep moving across this unending continent – even the very globe – for as long as the urge took me.

Unfortunately, Tay had no such luxury: his plane from Sydney left in two weeks' time and he had to be on a connecting flight from Cairns the day before it left. But the journey to Uluru tempted him; I knew he just needed a nudge. The chance came back in Cairns, when we passed a travel agency. Convincing him to go in and check whether he could depart from Uluru instead of Cairns, he came out a few minutes later, smiling. The trip was on.

The one note we received in reply to the car-share ads we'd posted on hostel noticeboards suggested meeting that lunchtime at the hostel reception. Whiling away the morning, we stumbled upon a free exhibition in town. It was of paintings by Brett Whitley, a well-known Australian artist who had died not long before, from heroin use. Tay's mother, who had also recently passed away from cancer, had been a visual artist, and perhaps her love of art had come down to her son: looking at Whitley's electrifying paintings and letters Tay was entranced. In front of one particularly vivid picture, his face lit up. Swept away by the moment, he exclaimed: 'My mother would love this one!' But as the reality of her death hit home, his face contorted into a scowl of pain and he remained in a sombre mood all the way back to the hostel.

Meeting the two ad respondents at lunchtime was like a reunion of sorts. I had met both girls previously in Brisbane, and so, skipping preliminaries, we jumped straight into preparations for our outback journey. Our travelling itineraries coincided perfectly, and as they had a tent, two of us could sleep under canvas and the other two in the car. Earlier that morning, Tay and I had bought enough food for four. We only had to buy more water to reach the recommended five litres per person per day for outback travelling, and we'd be off.

With everything concluded, we remembered that we'd neglected to do introductions. Turning to Tay, one girl held out her hand. 'Hi, I'm Avia and this is Kael. We're from Israel. We know Paul is from Ireland, but where are you from?'

I looked nervously at Tay, who had a 'to hell with it' glint in his eyes. 'Yes, nice to meet you. I'm from Germany. My mother was from Berlin and my father's Lebanese.'

Tay might as well have introduced himself as Heinrich Himmler. Avia and Kael's faces froze and they immediately stood bolt upright to leave. 'Paul, I think we need to talk about this between ourselves,' Avia said, very conspicuously to me. 'We will meet you back here in an hour to let you know. It was nice meeting you again.'

They shot out the door, leaving me and Tay in little doubt that we'd be travelling the desert alone.

I wasn't altogether surprised by their reaction. Backpackers tended to be in their twenties, recently out of college and still more children than adults. But Israelis, both male and female, had completed military service and grown up during violent times, and their experiences marked them out from most of the young travellers I met in Australia.

Shortly before, one night on Fraser Island, a twenty-three-year-old Israeli had confided hesitantly to our group that he had seen death during his military service in the West Bank. After a long pause, a drunken English backpacker threw out the inevitable question: 'And did you kill anyone, mate?'

He responded with a slow nod, and for some time we all stared silently into the fire.

Perhaps as a consequence of their war experiences, the Israeli men seemed years older than their female compatriots, most of whom had done their military service in administrative roles. They were certainly more mature than travellers from other countries. But Avia and Kael's vehement response made me inclined to believe that there might be some truth to the old adage that men start wars but women keep them going.

When Avia and Kael showed up an hour later to mutter, to me, a rather tepid excuse, I turned away in disgust. Australia was about young people opening up their minds to other cultures, and their obvious prejudices should, I felt, have stayed in the countries of the old world we'd left behind. But Tay was more sanguine. His complexion meant that, in Germany, he was often mistaken for a Turk and he was well used to racism. 'Shit happens,' he said with a shrug. 'Their loss.'

That afternoon, at the last minute, we picked up Pirita, a young Finnish student with chubby rosy cheeks, fair skin and white-blonde hair, and set off. Two hours after leaving Cairns, Pirita woke from her snooze, leaned forward between the front seats and remarked in her sweet sing-song voice: 'I think you're both very nice. I don't know why the woman in the hostel told me not to travel with you.'

'Why did she say that?' Tay asked pointedly.

'Well, she told me you were strangers and that you might rape me and leave me to die in the desert. But I don't think you'd be so mean. I think she was really silly.'

In contrast to his calm indifference to the day's earlier affront, Tay was fuming. 'The bitch!' he screamed. 'How dare she? Come on, turn the car around. Let's go back to Cairns and we'll get that bitch fired! Telling people we're rapists! She's never even met us!'

I mentioned to Tay that we were now almost two hundred kilometres from Cairns and should probably just let it go. Smoke came out his ears for the next ten minutes, but on we drove.

When we cut inland from Townsville onto the Flinders Highway, it was already dark. But wanting to put more distance behind us, we drove another two hours, stopping just outside the town of Charters Towers for the night. Used for so long to the salty scent of the ocean, we could now smell the warm, earthy air of the interior. Eating our late supper of fruit and soup we were like excited children, hardly able to wait until morning for our first glimpse of the outback.

Still piqued by being labelled a potential rapist, Tay offered up his sleeping place in the car to Pirita. But he was nervous of snakes and other night creatures, and instead of stretching out on the ground he grabbed a camp mat and sleeping bag and clambered up onto the car roof. A storm was brewing and the air was charged with electricity. Tired from our long drive, we thought nothing of it and lay down to sleep.

Despite the thunderous noise of Tay twisting and turning on the uncomfortable tin roof, we soon nodded off. But a real thunderstorm soon started up and, seconds later, Tay's large wet body hurtled in on top of us. He settled down across the front seats and, lulled by the sound of the rain on the roof, we all quickly fell asleep.

'Look in the side mirror,' Tay suggested to me the next morning as we woke to the sight of a yellow, rain-washed landscape. 'Maybe I should do the driving today.'

Leaning down to the side mirror, two badly bloodshot eyes reflected back at me; I had obviously strained them watching out for kangaroos the night before, and from the sun's glare during the day. (My prescription sunglasses were broken.) I gladly accepted Tay's offer; in fact, he was to do most of the driving the rest of the way to Alice Springs.

Our other discovery that morning was the phenomenon of blowflies. In all my outback travels I could never understand what I first encountered that day; how in this infinity of open desert, every square metre was choc-a-block with hundreds of flies ready to swoop down the instant you opened the car door. This pestilence, by necessity, makes outback cooking very quick and simple – not that you can rustle up much from a food supply of biscuits, tinned fish and vegetables. In any case, simplicity is best, as food has to be quickly gulped down to minimise the unwelcome garnish of sticky desert insect.

Soaking up the unexpectedly diverse sights of the desert, we drove for two hours – at which point the engine cut out. Seeing Tay and Pirita's concerned faces, I looked guiltily at the dashboard. I knew exactly what our problem was: we had run out of petrol. I had neglected to fix the fuel gauge, and it was obviously still on the blink. A breakdown in the outback was something new to me – and it worried me. I knew we had plenty of water and food, but the desert sun can be cruel, and distances between outback service stations can be vast.

With grizzly survival tales coming into my mind, I stuck out my thumb and was picked up by the second car that passed. Driving to the nearest servo – which, luckily, was only twenty kilometres down the road – the couple explained that they were coming from Darwin en route back home to Adelaide after spending seven months backpacking in Central America.

Still a little puzzled, I told them about the middle-aged woman who minutes before had averted her eyes as she drove by us. They exchanged an uncomfortable look, and then the man hesitantly explained. 'Yeah, you know what it probably was? Your mate, the dark bloke, he was out front, right? You and the girl weren't visible from the road, were ya? Well, she musta thought he was an Abo. Your car .... Well, ya see those old Holdens [Bertha looked similar to the Australian make], that's what those guys usually drive. She must have thought you were Abos.'

Ten minutes later they dropped me off at a service station that looked like something from a 1950s Midwest American movie. It had two rusty petrol pumps, a ramshackle shed and an old garage, above which a weather-beaten wooden sign read 'Torrens Creek'. On my map, Torrens Creek looked like a small town, but except for this ancient garage, all that was visible on the wide desert landscape were a few rundown shacks on the far side of the scorched road.

After peering through a grimy window into a seemingly empty garage office, I walked around to what must have been the workshop. Calling out, I stuck my head in, but all I could see inside were mounds of cannibalised 1960s and 1970s cars with their parts strewn on the ground. As I examined these relics, a trim, weathered man in his fifties, looking as composed as an elderly country priest, slowly appeared from behind an old truck. Despite the intense heat, his hair was neatly parted and his work overalls were buttoned up to the collar.

On seeing this stranger, he cleaned his oily hands with a rag and asked very civilly what he could do for me. I explained my need. Without a word, he walked out with me to the pumps and filled up my small fuel can with great care. After I paid him the few dollars, unbidden he stood in silence with me by the roadside as I waited to hitch a lift from the next passing car.

To make conversation, I asked him about the town. 'Used to be loads more houses along there,' he answered unhurriedly as he nodded ruefully across the road and barbed-wire fencing to the deserted bush. 'But that's the bloody Labor government [of Queensland] for you. A railway gang used to operate out of here, repairing the tracks, but the government reckoned there wasn't enough work, that it wasn't "economical", so they were all shipped off to another part of the state.'

For a long time, we stood side by side under the blazing sun in manly silence. Occasionally I'd glance westwards to see if a car had emerged from the shimmering heat. 'So how many people live here now?' I asked.

Pausing to think, he leaned back his head and, squinting up into the blinding, noon sky, began to count, ever so slowly. 'Two . . . .'

I was about to suggest 'hundred?' but then I saw that he was only starting. 'Four . . . six . . . eight . . . nine . . . eleven . . . .' Standing by those ancient petrol pumps, in the crucifying heat, a fuel can by my feet, I watched his kindly face fixed in concentration as he continued with his litany. 'Thirteen . . . fifteen . . . seventeen . . . nineteen . . . .' At twenty, he seemed to stop, as if the effort had completely worn him out. But then, with one last heave: 'No, twenty-one. Yeah, twenty-one.' With that he came to a halt, quietly satisfied that he had accounted for everyone in town.

A car picked me up shortly afterwards and, once I was back with Tay and Pirita, I threw a capful of fuel directly into the carburettor as Tay turned the ignition. Bertha started on the second go and we were back on the road again.

Filling up in Hughendon, we met a pregnant woman travelling with her husband and two children in a clapped-out Holden sedan. It was piled high inside and loaded with a solid, fibre-glass rowing boat strapped to the roof, together with a large trailer attached to the tow-bar.

'We've been travelling around the continent for a year,' the woman told us as we cooled down with cartons of iced coffee. 'My husband's a carpenter, so it's easy for him to pick up work as we go along, but now we've to head home to Philip Island – you know, where the penguins live, near Melbourne.'

'So you're heading into the Territories, yeah? Be careful, 'cos once you cross the border, it goes up by ten degrees.' We looked at her wide-eyed: in Australia that meant *Celsius*, so now we'd be travelling in about one hundred degrees Fahrenheit, without air-conditioning. 'And keep an eye out for 'roos,' she added. 'Some of those buggers are plain stupid. Especially the red ones. Just jump out at ya like kamikazes. Met a bloke down the road with a smashed-up ute [utility truck]. A big red bastard had just jumped in front of him, he said. The mechanic told him he needed a new radiator and it'd take two days to arrive, so he's rightly buggered.'

An hour later we saw the same ute on the roadside and were impressed that a new radiator was all that was needed to get it going again. It looked a complete write-off.

Nearing Mount Isa that afternoon, we felt tired, hot and grimy, and knew that only a night sleeping rough by the roadside awaited us. After travelling almost a thousand kilometres that day, I was itching to cool down. The map showed a lake just outside town, and I suggested to Tay and Pirita that we go for a swim. They didn't seem too keen.

'But aren't there meant to crocodiles in the water around here?' Tay asked nervously. Not willing to give up so easily, I suggested we ask at the local police station; if anyone knew of the local perils, it was bound to be them.

The well-groomed desk sergeant eyed us up with disapproval as we filed into his ordered, air-conditioned station in our dusty shorts and filthy T-shirts.

'Yeah, mate,' he responded dryly to our enquiry. 'Nothing in there except a few freshies [Freshwater Crocodiles].'

'Crocodiles, you mean?' I asked anxiously.

'Yeah, mate! But *only* freshies!'

I still looked unconvinced.

'Put it this way, mate, we've never lost anyone to 'em yet!' At that, he turned tetchily back to his paperwork.

That was good enough for me: twenty minutes later, I was wading through the thick undergrowth of Lake Moondarra as Tay and Pirita looked on from the banks, making cracks about strange shapes in the water and unexpected phone calls to Irish mothers. But after so long in the hot car, the swim was wonderful.

Looking back on it now, the relaxed attitude I had towards the real dangers of the natural world in Australia startles me. In Magnetic Island, I trekked with Tay through snake-infested terrain, with little hope of help if one of us was bitten. In Lake Moondarra, I could clearly see crocodiles only thirty metres away from me on the muddy banks. On Exmouth peninsula in Western Australia, I swam in shallow water murky with sand flicked up by manta rays. A piercing from one would have caused real pain; indeed, a sting to the heart from one killed Steve 'Crocodile Man' Irwin in 2006. Also in Western Australia – in Coral Bay – I waded in metre-deep water as a dozen reef sharks swam around me.

The risks I took travelling now seem reckless. But my thinking at the time was typical of that of any young backpacker. If thousands of people travel through these territories unharmed each year, why shouldn't I? And weren't you just as likely to be mugged when you arrived in a new city?

Australia is extremely rich in minerals and throughout the continent I was to visit several major mining centres. Mount Isa is one of the world's largest lead producers, and a huge supplier of silver and copper; it gave me my first real taste of these rough, male domains.

By six in the evening, there was already a group of very drunk miners in the pub, and a few drunken aboriginal women soon entered. As the men passed comments, the women approached them, occasionally tottering blind drunk against the men's bar stools. The miners bought them beers and began clutching crudely at their breasts and behinds. Watching them, it seemed like a scene between early white male settlers and Aboriginal 'gins' from two centuries before. Had anything changed in the relationship between the races in the intervening time? Not if the evidence before us was anything to go by.

As the last light left the sky, we drove back to the lake and set up camp in scrub near the water. Lighting a fire, we chatted about our journey since Cairns – which now seemed like weeks ago, even though we had left only the day before. Settling down to sleep early, we knew that if things went according to plan, we'd be stretching out on clean hostel beds in Alice Springs the following evening.

Alice Springs

A delicate ribbon of lilac lay along the horizon at five the next morning. With a long drive ahead of us, I roused the two others and we drove sleepily for two hours before stopping for a fly-infested breakfast at Camooweel. Knowing that we wouldn't see another servo for almost three hundred kilometres, we filled up and crossed the border into the Northern Territories.

This was our third day travelling in the outback and its infinite variety continued to astound us. Instead of the uniform, flat yellow or red scenery we'd expected, the desert alternated from flat to hilly, and from verdant green to ochre red to rich yellow. And unusual features continued to come into view, bringing interest to the panorama. That morning, for instance, hundreds of termite mounds, standing like two-metre-high headstones, were visible along both sides of the highway. Clustered together over such a wide area, they gave us the impression that we were driving through a vast desert cemetery.

Whatever about the changing landscape, the highway stayed constant. For hour after hour we'd chat, sleep, read or gaze out the window, but the road kept to its unending straight course as far as the distant horizon.

Four hours after entering the Territories, we reached Three Ways, a place well named. We had arrived from the east, from the Queensland coast; northwards led to Darwin; going south would bring us to Adelaide. We turned south, and at noon reached Tennant Creek, where, in the shade of a shop doorway, we ate an unappetising lunch of tinned tuna, baked beans and tepid water. The town – quite large by outback standards – seemed deserted; the only forms visible were haggard-faced Aborigines, who swished almost spectral-like along the dusty main road in the incandescent light of the midday sun.

An hour later, after stopping for a short while to trek among the Devil's Marbles, we spotted our first puncture – and groaned. The mysterious atmosphere of the Devil's Marbles' massive smooth granite boulders – explained in an Aboriginal Dreamtime as the eggs of the Rainbow Serpent – contrasted starkly with the sudden reality of having to change a wheel in thirty-seven-degree heat. Tay and I, anxious to be out of the sun, set to it like men possessed, lugging the gear out of the back, retrieving the spare, changing the wheels and repacking the car, all in a few minutes. Driving on, with only the relief of the thin current of warm air coming through the front windows, we used our dirty T-shirts to wipe the salty sweat from our necks, backs, eyebrows and eye sockets, so that we could at least see the road ahead.

As dusk approached, we spotted a broken-down car with three Aborigines standing around it, beer cans in hand. We were already cutting it fine if we wanted to get to Alice Springs before the kangaroos' evening feed near dusk. But remembering our experience when Tay was mistaken for an Aborigine when he tried to flag down a passing car near Torrens Creek, we pulled in. They were clearly surprised that we'd stopped – they had been preparing to spend the night out in the bush – and almost indifferently they accepted our offer to bring one of them to the nearest servo in Aileron.

An Aborigine, smelling of alcohol, got into the front seat and began talking aggressively while frequently swinging his arm in front of Tay's face to point out some feature on the landscape. Although he appeared to know the native place names, when he was asked about the Dreamtimes he didn't seem to know any. Some Dreamtimes are sacred – which might have accounted for his reticence – but the more he talked, the more I was convinced he simply knew little about his ancestral heritage.

This loss of connection with the land is in some ways the worst consequence of the white colonisation of Australia for Aborigines. In her book *Tracks*, which describes her trip by camel through outback Australia in the 1970s, Robyn Davidson wrote: 'No amount of anthropological detail can begin to convey Aboriginal *feeling* for their land. It is everything – their law, their ethics, their reason for existence. Without that relationship they become ghosts, half-people. . . . When they lose [the land], they lose themselves, their spirit, their culture.' Aborigines, quite simply, have been culturally and spiritually disembowelled.

The Mabo legal judgement giving Aborigines greater land rights, and a personal apology by John Howard for the 'stolen children' of Aborigines taken from their families earlier in the century, were prominent issues in these years. But despite the fight to regain their rights and retain their culture, in my outback travels I was mostly witness to Aborigines who seemed empty and who, zombie-like, sought oblivion through alcohol.

The first kangaroos had now begun to appear and by swinging his arm and blocking Tay's view, our hitchhiker was in danger of causing an accident. A little depressed by this dispiriting encounter, I wanted to offload our passenger and get to Alice Springs. But pulling into Aileron service station, the Aborigine urged us to bring him with us to Alice Springs. There, he said, we could all have a drink together. When I refused, he pleaded all the more. How about just one beer with him in the servo? Just one, *please*! Then we could drive on to Alice. I told him curtly that we'd agreed to bring him to Aileron and that we were now leaving. Abruptly, his tone became servile, his face fell and, thanking us politely, he disappeared off towards the service station.

As I filled up by the petrol pump in the dark, I saw that instead of going towards the lights of the shop, he went around the side of the building to slip off into the bush. It only struck me then that an Aborigine entering the servo alone might not be served alcohol at the counter. Perhaps that's what lay behind his earlier insistence on staying in our company.

We still had more than an hour left to Alice Springs. Tay dropped down to 80 kilometres per hour and sounded the horn frequently to warn any animals of our approach. In the pitch darkness, several large kangaroos bounded dangerously close in front of us, and later, two large cows suddenly appeared in our headlights, but Tay's sharp eyes saved us on each occasion, as he braked just in time. With thirty kilometres to go, and already anticipating the warm showers that awaited us, the car thumped over something on the road, and a loud rumbling started up from our undercarriage. Convinced that we'd driven over a large roadkill and were now scuppered just minutes from Alice Springs, loud curses filled the car. But on examination, we found that we'd passed over a discarded truck tyre. Despite the huge size of the tyre – and the grating noise – the car still moved. So on we drove, and finally, after setting out at 5.30 AM that morning, we reached Alice Springs and the end of our thousand-kilometre journey, just as the hostel reception was closing at 9.30 PM.

With Pirita safely checked into her room, Tay and I dumped our bags quietly near the three sleeping Japanese motorcyclists sharing our dorm. Peeling off our filthy clothes, we showered and were asleep by the time our heads hit the pillow.

In the last few decades, tourism has made Alice Springs a wealthy town: walking its tidy streets early the following morning, I could see it was no longer the town Nevil Shute described in *A Town Like Alice*. As Tay did his laundry and Pirita slept, I strolled alone past the new shopping centres, the cappuccino cafés and tourist shops stocked with overpriced aboriginal artworks. In an open area outside one boutique shop, a group of Aborigines sat under the shade of a tree, already drunk and cursing each other at ten in the morning. One middle-aged Aboriginal woman tried to get to her feet, but already legless, she just toppled backwards and fell down heavily onto the grass. Like the other nearby tourists, I just walked on.

Glad to stretch my legs again after three days in a car, I spent most of the morning wandering. From on top of Anzac Hill I gazed at the world's oldest mountain range, the 130 million-year-old MacDonnells, stretching out like a contoured spine east and west of town.

By early afternoon I reached the graveyard outside of town, and as the sun bore down I tried to decipher something of the town's pioneer past by the cryptic clues on the headstones. Occasionally going down on my hunkers to make out an inscription, I wondered what had brought these men to this Hades in the forgotten years before the Second World War? Unsurprisingly, I found no answer.

I did find Albert Namatjira's headstone, appropriately ornate, as the first Aborigine artist widely recognised outside Australia. But the graveyard's most ostentatious headstone belonged to Lassiter, a local man, who claimed to have found a huge seam of gold when he was out in the bush, lost. He set out several times – sometimes accompanied, sometimes alone – in search of this

El Dorado, before he finally vanished for good. But he didn't completely disappear, because with his passing the term 'Lassiter's gold', meaning a fool's dream, came into the Australian lexicon.

But we hadn't forgotten our appointment with Tim. We found him that afternoon sitting by a hostel pool, a drink on one side, a dark, attractive girl named Andrea on the other. 'Chaps!' he greeted us. 'So where've you been? I've been frantic.'

Andrea, like Tay, was only half German. Her father, an engineer, had met her mother while working on a project in Indonesia – which explained her exotic looks. Whiling away the afternoon, Tim leaned across to us discreetly. 'Lads, I was telling Andrea yesterday about our travel plans and was just wondering – do you think Bertha would be able to carry one more?' After an hour in her company, we'd warmed to Andrea, and so another passenger came onboard.

Uluru

Before leaving for Uluru, on Tim's suggestion, we set off the next day west-wards from town into the McDonnell Ranges. Tim told us that a bitumen road extends more than 100 kilometres westwards along some of the finest parts of the ranges, which, together with the Finke river system that runs through them, are the oldest of their kind in the world.

Arriving at Simpson's Gap, it seemed we'd arrived at a large sports venue given the number of tourists and tour buses. It was the same in Standley Chasm and Ellery Creek. But in both we had our first taste of the seemingly countless water pools to be found in the otherwise arid outback. Finding a rope hanging from a solitary eucalyptus tree, we swung high from it, to splash down into the cool waters of the lake. Drying off in the shade, a thrill rippled though our wiry bodies and it seemed that life could get no better.

Glen Helen Lake, at the farthest end of the sealed road, is enclosed all around by high rock, and the splashing sound as I resurfaced echoed loudly around the otherwise silent, stone amphitheatre. I enjoyed the calming atmos-phere of the place, and it was some time before I noticed four Aborigines perched high up on the surrounding rock looking down upon these strangers, shattering the stillness of their lake. Their skin was so dark, and the whites of their eyes flashed around so sharply, that I was reminded of the sinister staccato camera shots in the film *Picnic at Hanging Rock*.

Abruptly I sensed that I was a complete intruder, and felt deeply ashamed. The idea of trying to explain this land in geological terms, in western thought or in linear time, suddenly struck me as absurd. The fullness of these places could only be conveyed through the descriptions thousands of years of living in them had evoked in the imagination of the native people. Only through the apparent simplicity of the Dreamtimes, it seemed to me, could their pregnant atmosphere and multilayered meanings be fully explained.

Aborigines believe that the outback, far from being empty, is peopled by countless spirits, and that evening I knew it was true. Driving back to Alice Springs at sunset, far out into the desert, I saw giant waves of soft, turquoise light flowing in high, wide arcs out over the edge of the horizon. I knew that the waves were only visible in my imagination, but nonetheless for those ten minutes they were as real to me as the bitumen road before us.

How anyone could ever feel lonely here was suddenly beyond me, the place was just so inhabited, so *full*. In stark contrast to what I'd always imagined about the Australian bush, the land seemed to me the richest, the most replete place I had ever seen.

We camped that night near Kings' Canyon, about four hours past Alice Springs on the road to Uluru. Up just after dawn, we trekked to its ridges in the relative cool of early morning. Gazing down at its red, pink and magenta tinges reflecting off the precipitous rock faces, it wasn't difficult to understood why it is often compared to the Grand Canyon. But we didn't delay, and by 9 AM we were on our way – finally – to Uluru.

I had left Sydney in September mainly to avoid travelling in the outback during the full bite of summer. But now it was November and the continent's red centre was like a cauldron. Even in the shade, the thermometer by the ranger's office read forty degrees, or over one hundred degrees Fahrenheit. With no car air-conditioning, and sleeping most nights either in the car or under canvas, the heat was beginning to grind us down. But we had something special to look forward to that afternoon and, tired after our early start, I soon nodded off.

An excited shout awoke me from my snooze early in the afternoon. 'There it is!' Tay screamed, pointing almost directly ahead of us through the windscreen. 'Uluru. We've made it!'

Rubbing my sleepy eyes, I saw a vast resplendent shape rise up from the flat desert floor. Even from a distance of seventy kilometres, it stood out so massively in the landscape that we could hardly take our eyes off it until we reached Yulara, the tourist access-town about twenty kilometres from Uluru.

At sunrise or sunset the sun seems to bleed spectacular shades from the almost animate rock face of Uluru; it is said to 'glow' red, and either hour is the best time to view it. So about an hour before sunset, under a crystal-blue sky, we drove to the viewing area several kilometres away and cracked open a few beers in anticipation of the spectacle awaiting us. Arriving at the viewing area, we weren't disappointed.

A simple fact might help explain the scale of Uluru and why its gigantic shape so dominates the landscape of the Gibson Desert: its base, of three by two kilometres, takes two hours to walk around. The original colour of Uluru, which in the local language means 'great pebble', is in fact grey; oxidisation lends it its famous ferrous red. And instead of the uniform smooth rock texture which I'd expected, many craters pockmark the rock surface, giving it the texture of a giant Aero bar.

Uluru is not just a sacred place to the Aborigines, it's also a physical shelter. In times of severe drought, traditionally Aborigines would come from hundreds of miles around to live in the many caves and overhangs at the rock base. Even when the surrounding desert is as dry as a bone, water residues are to be found around the rock, attracting emus, kangaroos and wallabies, which in turn can be killed for food. The water also sustains roots and fruit which grow around the rock base and could augment the Aborigines' food supply.

A photograph I still have from that evening at the viewing point shows the five of us – a Finn, a Lebanese-German, an English guy, an Indonesian-German and an Irish guy – sitting on Bertha, each of us tanned and fit and smiling, as free as birds with this world-famous wonder behind us. It's almost like a picture of a bomber crew before the raid from which only a few of the young men return; to me, it freezes in time that moment of golden youth and adventure that is perhaps only fully experienced once and that can never quite be recaptured. From all my Australian travels, it's my favourite image.

Driving back in near-darkness to the campsite, and still awe-struck at the glowing monolith we had just witnessed, we decided that we would climb the rock before sunrise the next morning. And so as our irksome alarms broke the night silence at 4.20 AM, we dressed quickly and, still groggy, arrived at the national park entrance just as the ranger was setting up for the day.

Beginning the climb in inky darkness, we could just make out the faint outline of the rock before us. Tim had volunteered to come behind with the girls, allowing Tay and me to forge on to the summit before 5.52 AM, that day's sunrise. The darkness didn't make for optimal conditions, as one person a year is killed climbing Uluru, either by a fall or a heart attack; and despite the chain and metal posts bored into the rock, the first, almost vertical, section of the climb is generally considered the most dangerous part of the ascent. But after surviving Magnetic Island, Tay and I felt almost indestructible, and we scampered rapidly up the rock face despite being barely able to make out our hands in front of us.

Soon we reached the end of the metal chain and a flatter surface with white painted arrows, which were only just discernible, marking the way. In stark contrast to the utter silence at the rock base, ferocious winds now blasted around us. Crouching like First World War trench soldiers, we raced along the narrow ridges hoping not to be blown into the deep wind-hollowed gullies on either side. Just as the faint pre-dawn light appeared, I arrived at a metal plaque cemented onto some rocks to mark the top. Waiting the long minute for Tay to appear, I had a touch of the Edmund Hillary and Tenzing Norgay's, and almost felt as if I was the first person ever to have stood on this dark, wind-blasted summit.

Tay soon arrived and, with his characteristic exuberance, over the noise of the wind he yelled ecstatically into my ear: 'Twenty-two minutes, Paul! It only took us twenty-two minutes to climb.' That was impressive, as most of the guidebooks suggest taking an hour and a half. In such a wind – our windcheater hoods were whipping wildly around our ears – it was difficult to talk, so for the next few minutes we stood without speaking, taking in the panorama before us. We both knew this was the pinnacle of our magnificent journey together, and that it was something we'd never forget.

A purple glimmer along the thin, eastern horizon slowly grew stronger and unveiled what seemed like a lunar landscape. A Norwegian appeared in the darkness behind us, followed soon after by Tim, and together we watched as the sun rose fully over the horizon and cast a beautiful cloak of soft light over the cold darkness of the central Australian desert.

We stayed on the summit for another hour. But in the growing heat, the Babel of arriving European and Asian tourists made the place feel a little crowded, and we started down. Tim had climbed the rock in open sandals and his feet were now covered with weeping blisters. But he was unfailingly cheerful as, barefoot, we watched the stream of sickly-pale Japanese tourists, lathered in sun cream and wearing thin white gloves like snooker referees, pant up the rock. From the crest of the rock, we looked down at the car park. It was now bustling with cars and buses disgorging armies of tourists, whose dark ant-trails led right up to the rock base. Finally locating the car among all the buses, we were back in the campsite at 9 AM, heat-baked, sweat-soaked but exultant.

The following morning, just after dawn, Tay and I walked part of the path around Uluru's base. This was the last day we'd spend together, and he gave me one last laugh by doing a headstand on the path: 'So I can remember what it feels like again to be in the Northern Hemisphere!' I took a photo of him with Uluru in the background for him to send back to his father.

I dropped him off at the airstrip at lunchtime, just as I'd dropped off Pirita the day before. The next day I left Tim at the small airport in Alice Springs for his flight to Sydney. After so many adventures together, Tay, Tim and I had become good friends, and both goodbyes were heartfelt.

Now Andrea and I were the only ones left as we began our long, circuitous journey back to Sydney.

Leaving the Outback

It was now obvious, as we prepared to leave Alice Springs once again, that twelve thousand kilometres of highway and dirt roads had taken their toll on Bertha. The road-train tyre we'd hit arriving into town had punched a golf-ball-sized hole in the exhaust: the noise only stopped when I finally replaced it in Sydney. The fuel gauge still had a mind of its own; and now the ignition was slow to start. A mechanic in Alice Springs told me that I really should get the points and plugs seen to. But three female Swedish passengers had now joined us. And with four women impatient to get started, I caved in, deciding to get the car seen to in Adelaide.

The uncompromising heat in the Northern Territories had sapped us, and we were looking forward to the relieving temperatures and ocean breezes of the southern coast. But perhaps deluded by the vineyards and temperate surroundings of Adelaide – still more than a thousand kilometres away – we failed to appreciate that South Australia is the driest state in the world's driest continent. It was no surprise, therefore, that crossing the border into South Australia, three hundred kilometres south of Alice Springs, the temperature remained unremittingly in the high thirties.

Slowly however, the further south we drove and the later the hour in the day, the heat began to ease. I was already contemplating the luxury of an air-conditioned hostel room in Coober Pedy – that night's destination – when an oncoming police car appeared flashing its lights, the outback warning for an approaching 'oversize' road-train. Pulling over, we watched as a fifteen-metre-wide metal girder passed slowly by and swallowed up the whole width of the road.

That's when our trouble began. The motor had cut out when we'd pulled in, and now I couldn't get it started again. After a few minutes we gave up, but despite everything, everyone remained remarkably calm. The subtle pinks and reds of an outback sunset were softly draining out of the western sky, and we all sat back in the car, quietly taking it in. But it would soon be dark, and as appealing as a night curled up in the desert with Andrea and three attractive Swedes might sound, after two weeks of roughing it in the outback, all I really wanted was a good wash and a long sleep in a clean hostel bed.

We waited some time for a car to pass, and eventually an elderly couple pulled in. 'Have you enough water, first of all?' the lady asked sensibly as she pulled two chilled water bottles from their eskie (Australian for icebox). They had just visited their daughter, a teacher in an Aboriginal settlement a few hours north, and were now on their way home to Adelaide.

Her husband, a retired mechanic, had a quick look under the bonnet and, shaking his head, confirmed that the points were gone. He suggested bringing one of us to Coober Pedy and calling the NRMA from there.

He then looked me in the eye and spoke in a low voice, nodding discreetly towards the three Swedes chattering together nearby. 'You'd better stay here mate, best a bloke around. Girls in the desert alone at night . . . ya know?' Andrea and I exchanged a glance and immediately she filled a small backpack. She soon drove off with the elderly couple, leaving us to the sound of the wind and the birds twittering at the last light of day.

A little grumpy – and guilty – I lay down along the front seats and listened as the girls chatted and laughed outside. An hour later, a tap on the window awoke me and, as I rolled down the window, an ice-cold beer appeared above my head. Startled, I sat up and saw the girls grinning at my look of amazement. The road was scarcely visible but it seemed as empty and silent as before. 'My God,' I asked, cracking open the frosty as if it was nectar, 'where the hell did you get this?' At which they all burst out laughing.

'Three really nice people in a truck stopped a few minutes ago and asked were we OK.' explained Erika. 'Two boys and a girl. We told them we were waiting for a mechanic and our friend was asleep in the car.'

Johanna then jumped forward. 'They asked us to a party. They said it was about seventy kilometres from here, but we said we've to wait here, but thanks.'

'But the two boys were very friendly' Erika interrupted, taking up the story again, 'and they gave us four beers from their icebox, one for each of us.' I held up my cold bottle of Toohey's in salute to our kind Samaritans and took a long, cold gulp.

We waited two hours and nothing came. Just as I was about to suggest we settle down for the night, two truck headlights lit up the inside of the car like a spaceship. Springing up from my seat, I saw a very large man, the image of the actor John Goodman, lurch down from a high truck cab.

'Don't mind helping an Irishman in bother. I'm Ron,' he said, sticking out an oily slab of a hand. 'Ever hear of Blarney, in Cork? That's where I was born.' Ron had lost all trace of an Irish accent, having spent most of his life in South Africa and now Australia. He quickly flashed his torch under the bonnet and closed it again. 'Points buggered. Better tow her back and have a look at her in the morning.'

For the next seventy kilometres, as Ron towed the car back to Cadney Homestead, I sat steering in Bertha's front seat and nervously watched the tow-chain suddenly tug and slacken as Ron veered and braked to avoid the kangaroos zipping across his headlights. An hour later he pulled off the road into a field alongside the service station. 'Best park here, guys. I'll bring her over to my workshop in the morning and have a look. You should be able to sleep here'

Early the next morning I found Ron supping a large coffee in his office. 'All it needed was a change of points,' he informed me. 'Only cost a few bucks for parts, and the labour was about twenty.' Then he paused as if remembering something unpleasant. 'Tell me, what sort of NRMA coverage did you say you have?' When I told him 'ordinary' and not 'gold', he looked at me with real regret.

'Ah shit. See, that means I'm meant to charge you for the towing, and that's calculated per kilometre, and we came seventy Ks last night.' Tapping on his calculator, he looked up again. 'That's bloody two hundred and ten bucks.' He sat back heavily in his creaking chair to think. Although three hundred dollars was no small amount when backpacking, I could easily enough afford it, especially as I was relieved to know that the car was now all right. But Ron wasn't done.

'That's a fair chunk of money for you guys. I know you backpackers travel on a tight budget.' He stopped to think. 'Your friend, the girl, she rang in and said you were seventy Ks from here, right? Well, in the outback people often say a hundred Ks when they mean fifty, and besides it was a *girl* who rang it in. Women ain't great with distances, right? So let's just say you were only thirty Ks away. That would make the total charge a hundred and thirty dollars instead. What do you reckon?' Humbled by such thoughtfulness, I thanked him, paid and left.

We drove the hundred and twenty kilometres to Coober Pedy in high spirits, happy to be seeing Andrea again. We were also entranced by the bizarre, lunar landscape, chosen for scenes in films such as *Mad Max* and *Priscilla, Queen of the Desert*. But despite its barren appearance, the desert area is rich in gems, and Coober Pedy at that time produced 80 percent of the world's opals. I was curious finally to visit an opal-mining town after hearing so many stories from Tom, a bank friend, about growing up in Lightning Ridge, another mining town, on the New South Wales/Queensland border.

'Great place to come from, mate,' Tom would tell me on our nights out. 'Out in the country, playing footie, hunting 'roos . . . You're not really meant to hunt 'em, ought to have a licence, but everyone does it. Yeah, just generally mucking about. Only thing is, there's jack to do when you get older except drink. It's so hot in summer ya gotta stay indoors, so most people just live in the pub or the RSL.' (RSLs, for Retired Serviceman's League, are clubs widespread in Australia, which were set up for veterans after the First World War and are now open to all.)

Lightning Ridge is a world-class opal producer. and most people in town mined for a living. 'A bloke up there finds an opal, maybe worth a coupla K,' Tom explained. ' He sells it and mightn't go back to work till all the money's gone. Pubs do good business up there. Then of course ya can gamble. Knew one woman, found a gem. Some people reckon it was worth about twenty thousand bucks. She came to the RSL – I used to work there during me holidays – and in no time she'd pissed all her money away down the pokies [poker machines]. Mind you, people up there really are the salt of the earth, really look after one another. Not like down here in the city, where a bloke might as soon piss on ya as look at ya.'

Coober Pedy seemed in many ways similar to the place described by Tom –

Whitsunday
Islands, Northern
Queensland

'Infinite Spaces'
Rainbow Beach,
Queensland

Port Arthur Penitentiary, Tasmania (view from ocean)

Freshly cut cross to the thirty-five
victims of the Port Arthur killings

Gavin Duffy's cottage,
Port Arthur, Tasmania

Hell's Gates
Strahan, Tasmania

Termite mounds
near Queensland
and NT border

Devil's Marbles,
Northern Territory

The great
pebble – Uluru

Uluru viewing
point at sunset.
Tay, Pirita, Tim,
author and Andrea

Reflection pool,
ANZAC War
Memorial,
Hyde Park,
Sydney

O'Malley's Pub,
King's Cross,
Rob standing on left
holding beer, Rory on
far right, Eoin (with
author) kneeling

Opera House,
Sydney

Nullarbor
('no tree') Desert,
South Australia &
Western Australia

'A lost city?'
The Pinnacles,
Western Australia

'A world away'
Kalbarri,
Western Australia

Left: View from Oxer's Lookout, Karajini, Western Australia

Below: Monika and Rory, Yardie Creek Gorge, Exmouth Peninsula, Western Australia

Japanese Cemetery, Broome, Western Australia

Sun setting over Cable Beach, Broome, Western Australia

Old boab prison tree, Derby, Western Australia

Timer photo, with Detlef, Rory and Monika, Yardie Creek Gorge, Exmouth Peninsula, Western Australia

Windjana Gorge, the Kimberleys, Western Australia

Dusty and thirsty
after the Kimberleys.
But no humbugging!
A coldie with Detlef
and Rory, Fitzroy
Crossing, Western
Australia

Old Telegraph
Office Hostel,
Fitzroy Crossing,
Western Australia

'Arcadia' –
Katherine Gorge,
Northern Territory

but with one big difference. Many of the empty mineshafts around town had been converted into homes and buildings. With summer heat often as high as fifty degrees Celsius, they seemed to make for very cool, habitable dwellings. And it was in a mine converted into a hostel that Andrea had spent the night, she explained, when she met us looking freshly showered and well rested outside the hostel door an hour later.

As the three girls wandered off, Andrea gave me a tour of the hostel. Its rooms, which had low, curved ceilings, seemed to have no doors but were deliciously cool after the dry desert air. One adjoining mine had been converted into a tiny underground Catholic church, which had the hushed, ethereal atmosphere of a small Roman catacomb.

Back on the road that afternoon, we finally began to detect the warm scent of the ocean. Despite the sapping month of heat, I felt reluctant to be leaving the desert. The outback had affected me deeply; it seemed to be so nurturing and so vibrantly alive. Indeed, its impact on me was so strong I half suspected I might be suffering from heat exhaustion. But as the sun faded over Spencer Gulf, I braced myself for our arrival into Adelaide, and for the culture shock of returning to the first city I'd been in since Brisbane almost two months before.

The Southern Cities:
Adelaide and Melbourne

Adelaide is often called the City of Light, not only because of its good climate but also in honour of its founder, Colonel William Light. It was he who designed the city in a symmetrical pattern around the Torrens river in the late 1830s. As the capital of the only Australian state never to have had a penal colony, Adelaide was less touched by some of the crass aspects of convictism. The arrival of German Lutherans in the 1840s not only led to the start of the wine industry in the nearby Barossa Valley, but also enhanced the higher 'moral tone' of the city. This partly explains the reputation the city's inhabitants have as the 'wowsers', or 'stick-in-the-muds', of Australia.

But despite its staid reputation, I was immediately drawn to the city. With its tall, colonial buildings and charming atmosphere, I felt it was the most beautiful city I'd yet seen in Australia. Its relatively temperate climate, the wide impressive streets, and the elegant central city grid surrounded by green parks and the Torrens River, reminded me strongly of a European city.

It was now almost Christmas, and one morning in the stately General Post Office I wrote letters and wrapped parcels to send to family back home. Just back from the burning heat of the Central Desert, it was a strange experience to hear the melodies of 'Good King Wenceslas' and Alpine 'Silent Night's wafting through the hushed post office. On this, my second Christmas in Australia, it made me very nostalgic for northern climes.

We spent three days in Adelaide. We drove down to Glenelg, the genial sea-side town where the colony was originally founded. We also went on a tour of the Barossa valley, where we made a real impression. Piling out of our exhaust-clattering, twenty-year-old station wagon at the entrance to the wineries, we raised some eyebrows as we strolled in, clad in our grubby travelling clothes, to offer our expert opinion on the proprietor's wide range of wines. Needless to say, we returned to Adelaide empty-handed, but in high spirits.

The afternoon before we left the city, I had an interesting encounter. After a long walk around North Terrace, Rundle Street and the banks of the Torrens river, I sat down on a park bench in Victoria Square to read over a letter I'd written earlier that day. A few metres away, at the corner of the square, stiffly dressed commuters, sensibly carrying umbrellas – it seemed a little overcast – stood waiting for the tram to bring them home after their day's work. My eyes back on the page, I suddenly heard a loud voice above me. 'What are you reading, man?'

Gazing up, I saw a broad-smiling, gap-toothed Aborigine standing in front of me with a friendly look of curiosity.

'Oh, just a letter,' I replied, turning back to it.

'Now don't tell me!' he responded gleefully, oblivious to my attempt to ignore him. 'Your accent? No, don't tell me!' And his glowing smile gave way to a look of deep concentration. 'You're not a Pom, right?'

I shook my head.

'Canadian, no?'

'Irish!' he screamed in delight when I told him. 'You're Irish. Hey, my uncle's Irish too!' he called out, thumping his chest with pride and breaking out into an even bigger smile than before. I looked at his deep, dark skin and distinctive features, and knew that there was no way he could convince me he wasn't anything but a full-blooded Aborigine.

'Yeah, Uncle Pat. Pac-man!' he continued. 'He's from County . . . Tarone? Tirone?'

'Tyrone?' I suggested.

'Yeah, Tyrone' he shouted out jubilantly. 'County Tyrone, that's it!'

'That sounds about right,' I replied, chuckling.

He gave me a rambling explanation. From what I could gather, his Uncle Pat was one of the last of the ten-pound assisted passengers to Australia in the early 1970s and had ended up marrying this man's aunt.

He introduced himself as Peter. 'Irish, eh? You know those English,' he added, now that we had bonded. 'Their queen, now that woman I don't understand.' And he shook his head, greatly perplexed. (This was the year before Diana was killed and the royals were going through the worst of their family disputes, separations and divorces.) 'She wants to rule your country and my country and she can't even take care of her own backyard!' I laughed at the simple logic of it, as Peter continued.

'You know, those English, they done the same to your land as to mine. My uncle Pat, he went to London. You know Big Ben, the big clock? Yeah? Well, he planted our flag on the top of Big Ben and claimed it for our people. That's what the English did in my land and in your land. Stick a flag in the ground and then say they own it. So now we must own Big Ben, isn't that right?'

At that he let out a great whooping laugh, which was so infectious that it set me off too. Lifting back my head, I could see that several commuters were glaring at us. Peter was a little drunk – I could smell the drink off his breath – and enjoying himself so much he seemed oblivious to it all. Somehow, however, I couldn't help but feel that the disapproving looks were directed towards me. What was I thinking, encouraging an inebriated Aborigine to talk and laugh loudly on a quiet, respectable square on a midweek afternoon? But Peter was great company, and I really didn't care. Besides, I was all the more amused because I knew Peter was only spinning me a tale, giving his uncle Pat the limelight, even if the basis of the story were true.

It had happened during Australia's 1988 bicentennial celebrations, when some of the Aborigine leaders travelled to England. Wanting to show up just how ridiculous the English claim of 'terra nullius' – literally 'the land of no man' – was in 1770, in appropriating Australia for the Crown (when Aborigines had obviously lived there for thousands of years) they made their way to Dover, planted the Aboriginal flag on one of the famous White Cliffs, and claimed England as sovereign Aboriginal territory.

For the next half an hour, Peter had me in tears of laughter with his stories and the verve with which he told them. Finally he'd only let me leave after I'd promised repeatedly to visit his uncle Pat and his wife when I was in Melbourne: he'd scribbled their St Kilda address on the back of my notebook in huge block letters.

'Now you promise you'll go and see them?' he pressed me once more. 'Go to their house. Punch Pac-man in the guts and give Aunt Lena a big wet kiss on the lips!' And with that he burst into another raucous outpouring of laughter. Swearing to him I would, I walked back to the hostel with a big grin on my face, not only highly entertained by the last half an hour but also deeply relieved after all the sorry cases I'd seen that I'd finally had a taste of the reputed, but rarely seen, wild sense of fun and playfulness of the Aborigines.

Driving along the Great Ocean Road to Melbourne the next day, bitter winds swept straight up from the Antarctic, and the heat of the outback seemed long forgotten. Built as a relief work during the Great Depression, the Great Ocean Road is one of the prime tourist sights of Australia, with its spectacular cliff-side views over the ocean and the famous sea-stacks named 'the Twelve Apostles'. But I was feeling jaded from travelling for more than two months and seeing endless 'amazing sights', and now, huddled up against the damp weather, I just wanted to rest in one place for a while.

Our travelling party broke up in Melbourne as I decided to hang about for a few days, perhaps even to look for work. The Swedish girls, on a tight schedule, left for Sydney by bus with Andrea the following day. And I now found myself for the first time since the Whitsundays on my own again.

It was the Victorian Gold Rush of the 1840s that turned Melbourne from a small settlement town into the only city on the continent large enough to compete with Sydney for the position of federal capital after 1901. Indeed, it was to become so for several years until Canberra, a midway point between the two cities, was founded as the neutral new federal capital several decades later.

The city experienced great population growth after the Second World War, with massive immigration into the city from southern Europe, especially Greece. This influx came to lend the city an indisputably European air, as evinced by the cafés, trams and elegant stores which now line the streets of the small central city grid.

This wasn't my first time to Melbourne. I had flown down here for a visit the year before with my Melbournite girlfriend. From the top of the Rialto

Tower, the city's tallest building, we had looked down on Flinders Park Stadium (where Boris Becker went on to win the Australian Open later that week) and the famous MCG, the Melbourne Cricket Ground, where Ronnie Delaney won a gold medal in the fifteen hundred metres in the 1956 Olympics. But what I most took away from my first visit to Melbourne, and that morning on the Rialto Tower, was the very human story of the post-war immigrants to Australia.

'On a clear day you can usually see Tassie from here,' my girlfriend's mother had told me from the top of the tower. 'It's only about two hundred miles away.'

She then nodded down towards Port Philip, the city port, which was clearly visible below. 'That's where our family arrived in, in the early fifties. Ten-pound assisted passage from England it was.' On arrival she couldn't understand why kids laughed at her when she said she'd eaten pumpkin (as she figured turnips were) back home. 'You don't eat pumpkin,' they said. 'That's what you feed the pigs!' Australia never had post-war rationing.

I later met *her* mother, who told me about the immigrant experience from the adult's perspective.

'The Australian immigration people in England had promised us a better life in a new land,' she explained. 'But when we got here, they put us in derby huts – you know, prefabs – and for months my husband had to dig ditches.' As a war-hardened former Red Beret sergeant-major, he was less than impressed. The last holes he'd come across were wells in Greek villages which his platoon had liberated. The Germans had dumped bodies into them to poison the drinking water, which left them with the grizzly task of extracting the bloated corpses from the wells. Later, in Australia, she told me, he got into construction and 'did all right for himself'.

The lady's strong character – she was in her eighties when I met her – still shone through. She must have been tough, like all her generation of 'New Australians'. They'd left Europe knowing it was unlikely they'd see their family and friends again; indeed, she wasn't to see England or her mother again for sixteen years. That, it seems, was just the way things were.

But this time, arriving into the city at the end of my long journey, I was less inclined to go sightseeing. I had no urge to return to work either but, nevertheless, I thought it best to contact Len to ask him to retrieve my work suit, now stored in his garden shed in Sydney, and send it to the Poste Restante in Melbourne GPO.

I had heard that desert travelling can sometimes affect people deeply. But I was still unprepared for the startling impact such a relative short outback journey was to have on me. It hardly helped matters that I was reading Nadya Mandelstam's *Hope Against Hope*, about the labyrinthine nightmare of Stalinist Russia into which her poet husband had disappeared. But in either case, waiting for the parcel to arrive from Sydney, I found myself over the next week walking around the streets of Melbourne under a strange spell. I was in such a daze that I was hard pushed to do the simplest things, like buy a bus ticket or a loaf of bread in the supermarket. One afternoon, returning from Flinders Park after a long day's walk around the city, the fever reached a height and I experienced a vivid, phantasmagorical hallucination on a city tram.

Boarding the tram, the world suddenly ground to slow-motion as, like an automaton, I intensely surveyed the expressions of each of my fellow passengers. As the flickering light passing through the tram's grimy windows fell onto the passengers, their faces began contorting and distorting in front of me like something from a hall of mirrors. All their facial features started to morph: cheekbones, nose-bridges, jaw-lines, eye sockets, foreheads; even the very shape of their skulls protruded and receded before me. And for the fifteen-minute tram ride I felt like I was really glimpsing into the hidden worlds of everyone around me. But instead of seeing their true black or white, good or bad, Dorian Gray selves, being so fluidly formed, they seemed instead to be utterly indefinable and unfathomable.

The following morning, I seemed to return to the world. As if suddenly waking up from a deep slumber, I found myself at breakfast in the hostel dining room bantering with another backpacker. The fever had broken. But something odd had happened to me in the outback, and I was to live in its afterglow for at least the next three months.

But now I had to turn my attention to more mundane matters. Checking in the post office after a week, I found my suit still hadn't arrived. I rang Len.

'Oh, Melbourne was it?' was the laconic response from Sydney. 'When I hung up from talking to you last week I couldn't remember whether you'd said

Adelaide or Melbourne, so I thought I should just wait till you rang again.' I could almost see the smile on his face. He'd scuppered me. With only a few weeks to Christmas, it was unlikely I'd get a temp job down here. I'd have a better chance in Sydney, and he knew it.

'Suppose you'll just have to come back here now,' Len said. For form's sake I called him a bastard, but I was touched that he missed me. He responded by laughing. 'See you in Paddy's for a few schooners after work tomorrow so. Half five OK?'

Travelling via Canberra, I drove the full thousand kilometres to Sydney the next day. Walking into the pub just after 6 PM, Len and Tom greeted me as if I'd just come back from a weekend in the Blue Mountains.

'Hey Martinez, ya tight-arsed bastard!' Tom cried out indignantly from his bar stool. 'How 'bout getting us a beer? A bloke could die of thirst around here.'

It was good to be back.

Sydney: Year Two

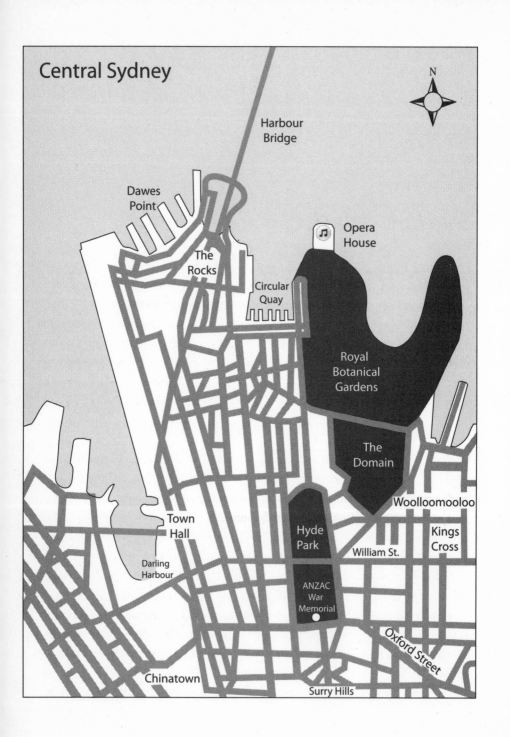

Sydney Again

Returning to Sydney, it seemed to have changed completely. In contrast to the chilly, grey streets that had greeted me on my arrival eighteen months before, the city was now filled with summer sunshine and happy faces in the lead-up to Christmas. But more than anything, it was not the city that had changed, but my circumstances. I now had friends here; I knew my way around; the streets and the celebrated landmarks were like familiar acquaintances rather than odd names to grapple with and decipher. Sydney, I pleasantly realised, now felt very much like home.

And as if in recognition that I was now on home turf, one phone call to the temp agency was enough to get me back into the bank. The section to which I was assigned was responsible for verifying credit card applications with employers and landlords. As the work was rather mundane, the staff was composed mostly of English and Irish temps.

One afternoon I heard a strong Dublin accent asking for everyone's attention, and I turned to listen. Looking very sullen, the temp announced that he was just back from the doctor and he had been diagnosed with measles. Presumably expecting a great wave of sympathy, the torrent of virulent abuse directed at him (mostly from female colleagues) clearly surprised him. Stunned by the uncharitable response, like an unwanted leper he left soon afterwards, muttering under his breath: 'So how was I meant to know measles can make a girl sterile?'

Not quite forgiven on his return a week later, Eoin visited me at my workstation. 'I heard you talking on the phone the other day. A southsider, eh? Ah well, we all have our crosses to bear.'

Eoin had come to Australia six months before, and glanced at me with respect when I told him I'd been here for a year and a half. I was now quite the veteran. Before returning to his calls, he mentioned that he was looking for one more person to share a new flat in Darling Point; if I heard of anyone looking, I should let him know.

And so I came to move in that weekend. The view outside the door was quite something, taking in Rushcutters Bay, the city, the Harbour Bridge and even, at a stretch, the Opera House. Each morning on the short walk to Edgecliff station, we passed the pretty Anglican church where Elton John had once married and which featured in *Muriel's Wedding*. Tom Cruise and Nicole Kidman, then still married, had a home just a few hundred metres up Darling Point road, and I later spotted Tom himself at the road junction in *Top Gun*-ish Ray-Bans driving a swish, dark sports car. It certainly was a great location.

But of course inside was a different story, as five young men – four Irish, one English – went about the business of living in a small two-bedroom flat.

Rob was quite surly when he found out about my new living arrangements. 'Oh, he doesn't mind roughing it *now*, when only last year he wouldn't even *dream* of sharing a room. If you'd left it with me, mister, I could have saved you a fortune!'

I tried to explain that like Scottish Andy after his circumnavigation of the continent the previous year, I now had the travel bug. And that if by sharing I could save more money and set off again sooner, it was well worth the discomfort. But Rob was thoroughly enjoying his I-told-you-so moment; only after I'd bought him a few beers did he gradually let it go.

At first I thought it a kindness on Eoin's part to allocate one room to just two of us, while he and two others shared the second room; that was until the first night. Then I swiftly discovered that Colin, my new roommate, snored in a truly spectacular fashion. So violent were his nasal emissions that they ricocheted about the tiny bedroom like acoustic cannonballs. Even when I tried to escape the nightly foghorn by pressing closely against the wall, I could feel the thin plaster vibrating against me. It continued night after night like a Chinese torture until a few weeks on, near collapse from sleep deprivation, I could take it no more, and was preparing to tell Eoin I was moving out. But then the police intervened in a most unexpected way.

Coming home from work one evening, I saw Colin standing in the hallway, clearly distressed. 'I've to return to Ireland straight away,' he blurted out before I'd even closed the door. Seeing the letter gripped in his hand, I braced myself for news of a serious family illness.

'I've been called for an interview with the Guards,' he explained. 'And if I don't go now, I mightn't be called again. Jaysus, what rotten luck!' Although no one had died, I was still choked with emotion. I shook his hand, wished him well and told him, truthfully, that the place wouldn't be the same without him.

After the great push to get approved credit cards into the hands of eager shoppers in time for Christmas, all the temps in our bank section were let go on Christmas Eve. Rather than being distressed, I spent a most enjoyable Christmas socialising and catching up with friends. And sure enough, I was back working in another temp assignment early in the new year, this time in a New South Wales state government department located near Sydney's Hyde Park.

Appropriately enough, given his striking resemblance to the comedian Russ Abbott, my new boss, Steve, was a born entertainer. Tall and pot-bellied, his booming, deadpan voice would regularly ring around the office with a wisecrack, all in the interest, he'd insist, of maintaining good staff morale.

Before working in the state government office, Steve had been a train driver on the Sydney underground. One day I told him about a suicide that had happened on the line the year before, which had caused my train to screech to a halt halfway between Edgecliff and Bondi metro stations. After a long wait, the driver instructed us to walk back through the train, jump down onto the tracks, and make out way back to the platform at Edgecliff station.

As we snaked our way through the train, the lights in only one small section of carriage were turned off. But despite the darkness, through the window I saw two police officers shine a torch onto a covered corpse as it lay inside the tunnel. A pair of white runners, attached to the two hairy calves sticking out from under the cover, flopped sideways and gave the sight an almost comical air. But then I saw several long red streaks along the wall and wondered, quite clinically, how the train had gathered enough speed, in the short distance from the station, to kill him so coldly and smear so much of his blood along the tunnel wall.

'If I'd experienced that as passenger,' I asked turning to Steve, 'it must be pretty rough on the driver.'

'You're right there, mate!' Steve answered. 'It can be a shocker all right. Worst thing about it though is you've to wait till the coppers arrive to inspect the scene and make sure it's not a murder.'

Steve had been the driver on two suicides. 'That wasn't so bad. One bloke in our garage hit double figures. No one would have a drink with him. Reckoned he was jinxed and the bad luck would rub off on us. People got to calling him "the Grim Reaper".'

After his first 'jumper', Steve headed over to his mother's. 'She knew something was up, I was that pale. I just looked up at her and said, "Mam, I got off early today, I just killed a bloke". And once the words were out of me mouth, the shock hit me and I started shaking like a bloody leaf.'

But it wasn't all bad times, Steve said. One April Fool's Day, as he was finishing his shift at rush-hour in Town Hall station, Steve hopped out of the driver's cab, disappeared behind the staff tea room and emerged seconds later leading the relief driver, who was wearing sunglasses and holding a white stick.

'Yeah, that's right mate, watch the wall, that's right,' Steve's booming voice rang out along the crowded platform.

'Watch the step! That's right, up you come.' Commuters looked anxiously towards the driver's cab as Steve and his colleague stepped up into it.

'Yeah, see this one, mate? The curved one, that's right?' Steve bellowed out through the open door. 'That starts the thing going, right? And this one over here, that's the one. Here, give me your hand. Yeah, that's right. That's the brake, all right? Yeah, it's dark for me too, mate, but I've got it figured out. It's about two and a half minutes – one hundred and fifty seconds – to Central station, so what I usually do is count it. Yeah, like one chimpanzee, two chimpanzee . . . ' 'Three chimpanzee,' his 'blind' co-worker joined in, 'four chimpanzee . . .' 'Yeah, that's right, you got the hang of it.'

Steve then hopped out of the cab onto the platform. 'Good luck so. Catch you for a beer after yer shift. Righto!' Just as the train was pulling off, Steve peeked his head around the corner of the tea room. 'And do you know what, mate? I watched the train pull away, and every one of them carriages was chock-ers – except for the one in front. Not a soul on board. That mob just stayed put on the platform. Must have decided to wait for the next train.'

As our English flatmate developed cashflow problems every rent day, I was soon sharing the flat exclusively with Irish people. After eighteen months of almost exclusively Australian and English roommates and friends, I found it refreshing to hang out with Irish lads again. And although it didn't compare with my first heady weeks in the country with Rob and Andy, the next few months remain a blur of barbecues, late nights and Irish bars.

Celebrating an office birthday one day, Steve looked at me earnestly and asked how the card sellers in Ireland were bearing up during these difficult times. I responded with a puzzled look. 'Well, they don't make cards for the eighteen-to-twenty-six-year-old market any more, do they? How could they, when every Irish person that age is bloody well down here?'

He had a point. With Ireland's star rising internationally (the term 'the Celtic Tiger' first reached Sydney around St Patrick's Day 1996) and with such an influx of backpackers, Sydney pub owners tried to cash in on their growing Irish clientele. The Henry the Seventh off George Street held Irish trad sessions; the Cock and Bull in Bondi Junction now called itself Siobhan's. Despite its name – and its tartan carpets – the York Tavern insisted that it was an Irish bar. (The St Patrick's Tavern, or Paddy's, the biggest late-night meat market in Sydney, was owned and run by Asians.)

Despite the frolics, I found that I was in many ways only physically back in Sydney. Although still at a loss as to what I would do when my Australian visa finally expired, my outback journey had bewitched me, and during those eight months back in the city my mind seemed to be mostly very far away.

In some ways, my job only sent me drifting off all the more, as it involved me talking with offices across New South Wales. Picking up the phone, I would visualise the small towns where the callers stood, the streets outside their windows, and the life and scenery all around them; and I longed to be there. But it was the regular calls from Norfolk Island that would invariably set me off in a daydream for the rest of the morning.

Norfolk Island, a small Pacific island a thousand kilometres off the

Australian coast, was a brutal penal colony where the most refractory convicts in mainland New South Wales were sent. It was also the setting for two of the rare uprisings against the authorities in early colonial times. The convicts, led by Irish convicts such as Dominick McCoy and Lawrence Duggan, were provoked into action more by the horrific conditions on the island than by any overt political aims. Norfolk Island was also the place to where many of the descendants of the Bounty mutineers were transferred in the 1860s. Pitcairn Island, their previous home, was considered so isolated that in comparison, Norfolk was viewed as being relatively accessible.

Anytime a call came through the switchboard from Norfolk, the caller invariably asked for the departmental manager. But my boss never took it; the caller always had a complaint, and my manager thought him a bore. But I never hesitated to take the call. What if the crabby man I was talking to was a direct descendant of Fletcher Christian?!

But it was letter-writing that, perhaps more than anything else, seemed to connect me to faraway places both in place and time. Rob had tried to introduce me to email just as the first internet cafés began to appear in Sydney the year before. But, as receptive as ever, I never took him up on it. (I only obtained my first email address in my NSW state job. And although it may have been useful during my many car breakdowns, I never had a mobile phone in Australia.)

However, I'm still deeply grateful that my period in the forgotten continent came just before the internet, mobile phones and social media gained such a hold over our daily lives, and that communications still took the form of a letter or short, expensive landline calls.

Several years after my return to Ireland, one Australian reminiscence involving new technology distressed me unexpectedly. 'It was amazing!' a girl told me when describing her trip to Uluru. 'The view, the desert, the climb and everything. And I sent a message to my folks at home right from the very top.'

I found myself appalled by the recollection. Not because I'm a Luddite, but because I felt that she'd wasted the experience. What was the point of travelling through the desert, absorbing all its sense of isolation, and then, the moment you arrived on the summit, thinking immediately about what people back home would think if they could see you now? Where was the 'dwelling in the moment'? Where would be the 'thought recollected in tranquillity'?

Perhaps this view was too purist, or more simply reflected what I wanted out of my time in the country; but even very frequent contact by phone to me seemed somehow to rupture the sense of isolation and scope for discovery that Australia offered. Alienation from the familiar is an essential part of travel; and perhaps occasional loneliness too. How else, I always thought, can you absorb new sensations and really learn?

Sending letters also meant that I received the occasional one in reply. And coming home to that handwritten envelope – handling the paper; trying to guess the sender from the writing, the country stamp, or the address; and reading the letter page front and back, and then reading it again – seemed to connect me to former generations.

The more daily minutiae the letter contained, the more it reminded me of my previous life and that someone cared enough to recount it to me. In the intimacy and the warmth that came to me from those envelopes, I felt as if I were sharing what earlier immigrants to Australia must have felt when a carefully inscribed letter reached their isolated dwelling with news of family or business affairs from 'your faithful friend' in the land they'd long left behind.

This Quixotic life

Trying after my travels to settle back into a working life, I found myself in these months pouring my restless energy back into books, and into obsessively remarking upon them in my diaries.

Ever since landing in Australia a year and a half before, I had been reading voraciously. In sunny parks, in crowded trains, in Spartan bedrooms and airy cafes, my head was always stuck in a book. Unfailingly, each Saturday I'd browse the second-hand bookshops in Glebe near Sydney University. During the week, after work, while Asian English-language students dozed on top of their grammar books all around me, I'd spend several hours reading or perusing the bookshelves in Town Hall Library. Any moment I could shave off the day – eating alone, at a bus-stop, during short breaks in work – I'd read. At times it seemed like the only justification I had for my otherwise rather nebulous existence.

I'd set out on my reading adventure in the spirit of the Russian poet, Boris Pasternak's verse from 'The Last Summer':

> Into obscurity retiring;
> Try your development to hide
> As autumn mist on early mornings
> Conceals the dreaming countryside

But it was evident from my hallucinations, both at sunset returning from the McDonnell Ranges near Alice Springs and later on the tram in Melbourne, that my outback journey and all that had gone before had affected me deeply.

Now back in Sydney, I felt as if a retaining wall had been broken down inside me and that the vast, vivid, light-filled world of Australia was crashing in on my mind. With it, the act of reading had now become unimaginably sensual for me. Each morsel, each sentence, every flicker of meaning seemed so delectable that I now almost quivered with pleasure each time I picked up a book.

So perhaps it was no coincidence that around this time I enrolled in a Latin-American literature course. The teacher, Raphael, was a fiery Peruvian writer-turned-teacher who exuded an electrifying passion for literature. Being so volatile and absentminded, he once admitted, that he didn't drive; he knew he'd cause too many accidents. Here, it seemed to me, was a true artist.

And in one of his many volcanic outpourings he told us that giving Spanish language lessons bored him to tears; they simply paid the bills. All his pent-up energy he saved for his writing and for our weekly literature class, when his observations about books would pour out of him in torrents. For the next three months he grabbed and hurled us through a roller-coaster ride of passionate, incisive glimpses into the world of Latin American literature and politics. He told us about the continent's turbulent history and lifestyle and introduced us to Borges, García Márquez, Mario Vargas Llosa, Isabel Allende, Julio Cortazár, Octavio Paz and other of the better-known Latin Americans.

'Borges,' he'd rave, 'his mother, she go into his room when he go out and read his manuscript and change a few words. He come back and see the changes and he go mad, crazy! They fight and argue and scream about words and tone and commas. About literature. But you know, she was the only person he really listened to about his writing.'

Although he worshipped Borges the writer, that didn't stop him making exuberant, vaudevillian fun of him as a molly-coddled son. 'At her funeral,' Raphael cried out, fingers crawling down his face, 'this man goes *boo hoo hoo*, his face full of tears when his mama dies. Only then a few months later, the only woman of his life now gone, does he finally marry. His age? Seventy-two!'

Julio Cortazár, whom he also revered as a writer, he told us was ''orribly ugly!'; a recluse who hated the world but who wrote to perfection! In Lima, Raphael had known the son of Mario Vargos Llosa and would tell us about the writer's habits at home, his failed run for the Peruvian Presidency and the punch-up he once had with Gabriel García Márquez.

But Raphael's frenzied tutelage wasn't all reserved to gossip and through him the Latin American writers hit me like a thunderbolt. Perhaps it was because they tapped deeply into instincts my recent outback travels had set loose. But the inner life, as they presented it, seemed inexhaustible. And despite all the brutality and suffering in their history and their politics, they portrayed the world as a place gleaming with beauty. In stark contrast to the seemingly perennial European lamentations about the emptiness of the quotidian, they stressed the imperative of harmoniously engaging in all aspects of life and thought. All else seemed simple foolishness.

Just as I associate my mauve-painted bedroom of the previous year in Leichhardt with the Russians, those eight months in Darling Point evoke in me the Latin-American writers and sunshine, and sitting on the grass in Hyde Park across the road from my work near the War Monument. If the bus was early in the morning, or at lunchtime, or after work, I read there, occasionally looking up at the sapphire sky, dizzy with reading, and wondering about the world.

However, my initial plan of escaping to a distant country to read as free as a bird had, almost imperceptibly, extended from one year to two. And still I felt reluctant to move on. My bridging visa had been issued in July 1996, and I could only hope for it to last just over a year. It was now early 1997 and I simply had to complete this nonsensical task I'd set myself – to read and realise something deep about my life and the world.

But no matter what or how much I read I was never satisfied. In a biography of Albert Speer, Hitler's architect and industry minister, I read that in his nine years in Spandau prison he read one thousand five hundred books – over three a week. And in his mostly autobiographical 1935 American novel, *Of Time and the River*, Thomas Wolfe's narrator claimed to have read twenty thousand volumes in the space of ten years. I just couldn't compete.

I envied Borges his librarian job in a drab Buenos Aires suburb. Working at a steady pace, he catalogued four hundred books on his first day. But his colleagues reprimanded him for working too hard; if he kept that pace the cataloguing would soon be finished and they'd be out of jobs. So for the next seven years he catalogued books for an hour each morning before retiring to the basement where he'd read and write for the rest of the day.

With similarly undemanding work I channelled my spare mental energy into pondering every snippet I'd read, and at my work computer I would write with great distillation about what I was reading. But despite the exquisite pleasure I now derived from literature, after several months back in Sydney I felt as if I were still in a cluttered, dark wardrobe. After two years, why couldn't I break through into the magical, sun-filled Narnia-like land which, like a demented archaeologist, I was utterly convinced lay beyond?

But despite my utter absorption in books – I was probably now, like Speer, reading three a week – I seemed to realise that I was living in a netherworld. It was as if the boundary between my daily world and the world of my reveries had been breached. The life I was now living somehow wasn't quite real.

Dreaming away one evening in class, I heard Raphael rattle out two questions in his customary way. 'The division between life and literature,' he asked. 'Where is it? They say there are two great victims in literature, who are they?'

Ignoring our attempts to answer, he replied himself. 'Madame Bovary and Don Quixote! Madame Bovary because she was the victim of crazy romantic novels and tried to make every lover like a hero of one of her books, wearing them all out with her suffocating zeal. And it was the cause of her downfall. And Don Quixote because he lost his sense of reality to books of chivalric tales and went off to lead that life at least a century too late.'

This observation made me sit up. Perhaps I was acting a little like Don Quixote myself. What was I now doing, except tilting at windmills?

At the front of my diary from these months I see that I transcribed a stanza from Victor Daley's poem 'Dreams'.

> I have been dreaming all a summer day:
> Shall I go dreaming so until Life's light
> Fades in Death's dusk, and all my days are spent?

When, I began to wonder, would I ever come to my senses?

What's another year?

Reading *Seven Years in Tibet* I'd always felt there was something amiss. A great adventure story it is, but in describing so many years of wandering in Asia only once, as far as I recall, did Heinrich Harrier make any reference to missing his family or friends back in a Europe then being decimated by the Second World War. Something didn't ring true. Only later when his Nazi connections were revealed did the emotional lapse seem to make sense. Unable to tell the full story, he had presumably also filtered out his experience of longing and loneliness that are an essential part of travel.

What people 'back home' thought young people were doing in Australia always seemed simplistic to me. Believing that young people go to such a distant country only to drink beer in the sun for a year seemed to miss the point. And talking the matter over with Eoin and my new Irish flatmates I only became more convinced of this view. Although backpackers certainly weren't living like Trappist monks, there was always something more urgent and serious underlying why they were here.

As has faced many generations of Irish people, unemployment was rife when we finished our studies in the early 1990s. The economic upturn was still a few years away; and, like me, my flatmates had come out of college when unemployment reached as high as 16 percent and most of the available jobs seemed to have been dead-end and miserably paid.

So what was there to hold us? Ireland was where we came from and where our families and many of our friends lived. But having grown up through the endless recessions and seeming inertia of the late 1970s, 1980s and early 1990s – when announcements of factories and businesses closing were daily occurrences – we had long since been taught to feel that Ireland had little to offer.

With such low expectations and such ambiguous feelings about Ireland, few of us down in Australia were weeping into our pints. Working in sunshine seemed much better than the alternative in Ireland. But being on one-year visas, with little chance for most of obtaining permanent residency or even extended visas, most backpackers in Australia felt like they were living on shifting sands, which were now quickly slipping through an hourglass. The year would soon be up and what would we do then?

Perhaps that explains why, in my experience, loneliness really hit people after they had secured extended visas or stayed on illegally. One year of fun and novelty tends to pass quickly and shields most people from homesickness. But as backpackers swung into their second or even third years away, and having traversed such huge distances, many appeared lost and adrift, both physically and emotionally. How could they explain to people back home just how far away Australia can seem, or the reasons for wanting to stay – for not wanting to return – in anything more than a hackneyed phrase? Unable to explain the oddness going on inside their heads, often people couldn't seem to cope, and many turned a little strange.

A common reaction was to drink heavily. While drunk, they would lament excessively about the negative aspects of home, thereby revealing all the more their longing for distant family and friends. Others, who had been happy drunks in their first year, often turned unpleasant, picking fights with close friends on the slimmest of pretexts.

Others took to odd behaviour. One acquaintance began to disappear from friends in the pub just when things were in full swing to taxi down to a local RSL. There he'd play the pokies for hours, only leaving, generally broke, around dawn. Another, dealing with an unpleasant, but not unusual, break-up later told me that, unable to cope without having family support nearby, he had seriously contemplated jumping off the Harbour Bridge.

But the most usual reaction was to simply detach from the world, to just shut down. The person's eyes would become vacant, and although perfunctorily civil, they would answer questions with monosyllables so that their company became like that of a corpse.

Having seen no close friend or relative in almost two years, about this time I responded in the same way. Looking in the bathroom mirror one morning I was sure of it. I'd seen those eyes before, in Irish bars in London and the States, and in Dublin in the late eighties and early nineties, in the faces of emigrants back for Christmas. I remembered those glazed eyes; taking in all the bustle and merry activity around them but knowing sadly that they can take no part in it now; that they no longer belong.

I've heard it said that 'home means never having to explain yourself'. And that's how I now felt. Punch-drunk from all I'd witnessed, read and pondered since coming to Australia, I felt as if my connection with the world had been broken, and I could do nothing to pull myself back. The only thing I remember with any clarity from those few winter months was sitting, seemingly for hours, staring into the large reflection pool by the War Memorial in Hyde Park. Lying back on the grass I'd then gaze up at the infinite sheen of the sapphire sky, and wish to God I could just switch off.

I had made some close friends in Australia, but now I felt exhausted. I no longer wanted to explain myself to people who knew nothing of me except what they'd learnt in the last two years. Now I just wanted to sit quietly with someone who'd known me for years, who knew the people, the places and the 'me' of my past life. I wanted to soak up the pleasure and affection of long friendship – without uttering a solitary word.

These emotional responses might sound extreme. But as Captain Joshua Slocum wrote when he sighted land towards the end of his 1890s' solo voyage around the world: 'I slid down the mast, trembling under the strangest sensations; and not able to resist the impulse, I sat on deck and gave way to my emotions. To folks in a parlour on shore this may seem weak indeed, but I am telling the story of a voyage alone.'

Ironically, it was around this time, in the southern winter of 1997, that I received one of my first emails at work; it was from Rory, a college friend. He asked if I was still in Sydney, as he was thinking of coming down, and wanted to know if I could put him up for a while. Rory had also been thinking of coming with me to Australia two years before, so, not holding my breath, I replied blithely that I was and there would be no problem putting him up, we had loads of room. In this new world of almost instantaneous communications – with the time difference I read his email the next day – a droll response came back.

'You say there's loads of room. If I remember that's what you once told your brother before he came to visit you in Munich, not knowing that you were then sleeping rough in the central train station. Please tell me that you are now actually living in a proper flat.' Smiling that someone knew of my existence before Australia, I immediately assured him that I was.

He arrived that June, another mattress went on the floor, and life resumed its languid pace. We quickly introduced him to many of the drinking establishments around the city. Eoin helped him get a job and he soon settled in.

I'd been on my bridging visa now for a year and although the system was jammed up with the high volume of applications, I knew I really couldn't expect to have much more time before mine was reviewed – and almost certainly refused. I had eight thousand Australian dollars now put away in the bank and I knew it was time to travel. I had set my sights on Western Australia, or WA, as the last part of the continent I had to yet visit. But when I proposed he join me, Rory seemed quite hesitant.

'But I've only just got here. And I've just got a decent job. Why would I throw it in and go travelling?'

'For the adventure,' I suggested. 'And travelling to WA by car is the only way you can really do it.'

'But why would I want to drive all the way across to Perth when I've already paid for three internal air-tickets?'

I hadn't considered that one and I paused a moment. It was now or never. 'How about I drive the car across to Perth and pick you up there?' With a little more convincing, it was soon agreed. And so that July I found myself setting off from Sydney to drive four thousand kilometres alone across the continent to the shores of the Indian Ocean.

Across the Continent
to Perth

Across the Continent
Sydney to Perth

N

INDIAN

OCEAN

Darwin

NORTHERN

TERRITORY

QUEENSLAND

PACIFIC

OCEAN

WESTERN

AUSTRALIA

Alice Springs

SOUTH

AUSTRALIA

Brisbane

Kalgoorlie

Nullarbor Desert

9

NEW SOUTH

Perth

11 10

Ceduna Port Augusta

WALES

Blue
Mts

12

Mildura

3 2

Great
Australian
Bight

4

Sydney

Adelaide

Canberra

VICTORIA

Melbourne

SOUTHERN

OCEAN

Hobart

TASMANIA

1. Sydney	5. Mildura	8. Ceduna	11. Caiguna
2. Bathurst	6. Adelaide	9. Nullarbor Roadhouse	12. Norseman
3. Cowra	7. Port Augusta	10. Cocklebiddy	13. Kalgoorlie
4. Hay			14. Perth

0   1000kms

Down to Adelaide

Leaving Sydney this time seemed different, more final, than when I'd left to go travelling the year before. Although Rob and Len were staying put, my Darling Point flatmates and yet another set of backpacker friends would have left by the time I returned to the city. Although by now I was used to these regular departures of acquaintances, after two years the intransience of this backpacker existence was beginning to get to me.

Earlier in the week when I'd checked with Immigration whether I could return briefly to Ireland for a family wedding and then re-enter the country on my bridging visa, I was quickly put right. The 'loophole' by which I'd obtained my bridging visa, I was told, had been tidied up the previous October and so the answer to my inquiry was a curt 'no'. Departing this time, I knew I was now effectively leaving Sydney for good. Whenever I did return it would only be to pack up my belongings and board a flight out of the country.

So it was in a particularly thoughtful mood that I set off over the Blue Mountains that Saturday morning on my route down to Adelaide, the mid-point on my journey to Perth. That autumn had been unusually dry, and crisp winter sunlight slanted across the brown, almost cindery countryside. Feeling heavy with tiredness after my send-off party the evening before, I listened to a reading of Wilfred Owens's First World War poems and final letters on my muffled tape player and brooded sombrely about the impermanence of this life I was leading and the long road ahead of me.

I stopped that evening to eat in Bathhurst RSL. Inside it was warm and welcoming, and, worn out after my drive, the food tasted hot and filling.

Sitting over my plate, I took in the friendly, ruddy faces and the kind familiarity of the country people chatting at the tables around me. It reminded me of arriving into another small community, at Hobart airport, the year before.

. . . *A year ago*! I thought. My God, so long?! How was Helen, my Leichhardt roommate, getting on in London? I wondered. She had brought me here to Bathhurst, her hometown, the year before. I smiled at the thought of what she must be up to in the house she shared with a bunch of Aussies and Kiwis in London . . . in Europe. It all felt so very far away.

But then so did Perth. One knowledgeable Sydney backpacker had told me in the pub the night before that Sydney to Perth was the same distance as going from London to Moscow. On my trip the year before I'd racked up eighteen thousand kilometres, so I knew Bertha could make it. In my drained state, I just wondered, could *I*?

But my most immediate concern now was leaving the warmth of the RSL. Coming into Bathurst, the crest of the Blue Mountains had been haloed in pink, the only brightness in an otherwise pitch-dark sky. So I knew it would be a bitterly cold night. And after promising myself before I'd left Sydney that I'd sleep in the car on this transcontinental journey, I knew I'd feel every freezing moment of it, too.

After an hour, I tore myself reluctantly away from the rosy-cheek warmth of the RSL and a few kilometres outside town pulled in along a quiet roadside. Putting on every stitch I'd brought – a pair of jeans, a tracksuit, a T-shirt, a sweater, an overcoat and two pairs of socks – I jumped into my sleeping bag, covered myself with a blanket and then spent the coldest night of my life.

Shivering for most of the hours of darkness, only at the first traces of dawn did I manage to finally nod off. Still frozen when I woke up at eight, my numb fingers could barely put the key in the ignition, let alone turn it. Warmed slightly by the yellowy winter sunlight reflecting off the ground's blanket of frost, I managed to clear a peephole in the iced-up windscreen just large enough to allow me to make my way precariously into town in search of a hot breakfast. Thawed by several scalding cups of tea and a piping full breakfast, an hour later I finally felt human enough to walk a little around town.

Bathurst really is a delightful place. Founded in 1832 shortly after convicts had completed the first road over the Blue Mountains, it was the first inland city in Australia and played an important role in opening up the interior to new settlers. Elegant and quaint, its wide streets are lined with tall, wrought-iron lamps harking back to when Queen Victoria reigned, gas still lit-up streets, and horse-drawn vehicles could circle in the town's wide streets with ease.

In keeping with the colonial tone, the plaque on the Boer War memorial in the main square in front of the classical courthouse and music conservatory intrigues. General Kitchener himself unveiled the monument in 1910. Standing in the frosty air, I wondered what could have induced such an important personage of empire, then at its height, not only to come to this far-flung (and by then former) colony but also to make an arduous journey over the mountains to open this obscure war memorial.

Leaving town in the mid-morning sunlight, the surrounding countryside seemed softer and warmer, perhaps reflecting my mood as much as the landscape. But that changed as I came to Cowra, a small rural town indelibly marked by an event that took place there on 5 August 1944. On that day, more than a thousand Japanese POW's escaped from the town's prison camp. A slaughter soon ensued as over two hundred Japanese and four Australians were killed before the prisoners were all recaptured.

The rows of headstones in the tidy town cemetery, many belonging to the escapees, are etched with neat Japanese characters. The night before had shown me how bitterly cold winter nights could be in these parts and made me wonder all the more why the Japanese had attempted such a hopeless breakout. Even if they survived the cold and exposure, the coast was hundreds of kilometres away across the mountains. It seemed an act of desperation, like the convict escape attempts into the Tasmanian bush. Both seemed destined for almost certain recapture or death.

Although I'd only driven five hundred kilometres that day, the idea of spending another night in the car was too much to contemplate, so I checked into a motel in the town of Hay. After a long shower, I leapt under the electric blanket and thick covers and slept soundly, little knowing that this would be the last real comfort I'd experience for several months.

The next day at noon, I arrived at the wide Murray River which forms the border between New South Wales and Victoria – I was now entering Ned Kelly country. It was near here in the Gelda district of North Victoria that in the 1870s Kelly rode wild, robbing mainly the better-off and becoming the common man's bush Robin Hood.

Kelly's father, John 'Red' Kelly, had been transported to Van Diemen's Land from Tipperary in 1842 for pig stealing and his mother, a fiercely independent woman, was a free emigrant from the west of Ireland. Although he could be cruel and vicious, his background bred into Ned the strong belief that he had social justice on his side and that he was fighting for the downtrodden class of the freed Irish convicts and settlers, to which he belonged. It's small surprise therefore that he loathed the ruling class with a vengeance for treating his people, the Irish, like swine – just as they'd spat on them in Ireland.

Accordingly, Kelly saved his worst spleen for any Irishmen who served the authorities. These 'turn-coats' had, he wrote in his famous letter from Jerilderie, a town in New South Wales, which his gang held up for several days in 1879, 'for a lazy loafing cowardly bilit left the ash corner, deserted the shamrock, the emblem of true wit and beauty to serve under a flag and nation that has destroyed massacreed and murdered their fore-fathers by the greatest of torture.' The ruling classes, he said, were little better, being a 'parcel of big ugly fat-necked wombat-headed big-bellied magpie-legged narrow-hipped splay-footed sons of Irish Baliffs or English landlords'.

It's ironic, then, that it was Irishmen who brought him down. He was sentenced to hang for the murder of a deputy named Lonigan, whom he claimed had once dragged him across a street in Benalla by his private parts. Senior-constable John Kelly was one of the three men who captured him, by firing not at his famous suit of armour but at his unprotected legs. And Justice Redmond Barry, a graduate of Trinity College Dublin, was his hanging judge.

But Ned Kelly was a vastly popular figure, and two days before his execution in the Melbourne Penitentiary in 1880, four thousand people crowded into the city's Hippodrome (as two thousand more waited outside) in a vain bid to persuade the Governor of Victoria to commute his death sentence.

Kelly had guts, and style. When Barry pronounced his death sentence, Kelly replied, 'I will see you where I am going.' Less than a fortnight after Kelly was hanged, Barry died from a carbuncle on his neck, which only added to the legend. As he was being led to the gallows, Kelly remarked upon the pretty flowers in the jail garden and, seeing the rope, spoke his famous, stoic last words: 'such is life.'

For those eking out a harsh existence in the uncompromising land of Australia in the 1870s and 1880s, it's little wonder that a man who lived, and died, in such a spirited and courageous manner was lionised throughout the continent – and still remains the most written-about person in Australian history.

Driving alone over the soft winter landscape for those few days, I ruminated about my time since coming to Australia. And as I did so, and the nearer I came to the South Australian capital, the more I found my mind drifting back almost a decade to Italy, and to Anna, the only Adelaide person I'd met before coming to Australia.

I'd met her one college summer in Milan while sharing a flat with a group of bohemian English teachers in their late twenties who seemed to have stepped out of a Hemmingway novel.

Alan, a poet's son from New England, wore John Lennon glasses and lent me his copies of Borges and Gide. Sinead, his kind Irish girlfriend, tied plastic windmills to the balcony railings and explained how she wanted to set up a balloon store in Nantucket. Steve, the Midwestern American, strummed his guitar late into the night, talking to me about Heidegger and Wallace Stevens, about his time as a nurse in a psychiatric hospital and how his malicious mother had delayed calling the ambulance after his father had shot himself.

Proust once wrote that 'what attracts people one to another is not a common point of view but a consanguinity of spirit'. And this might partly explain why, even among all these colourful characters, Anna in her quiet way seemed to me far more remarkable. She had travelled alone across Asia on the Trans-Siberian Railway when the USSR still stood (Sinead had told me this; Anna would have been much too modest to mention it). Speaking several languages fluently, she had then worked in several European countries and was now teaching English in a language school in Milan.

She also read voraciously. Whenever we arrived, usually late, to meet her at the arranged rendezvous in a piazza or at a metro entrance, she'd look up genially from the novel she had just been reading in French, Italian or German and never utter a word of rebuke for our tardiness. Affable and gracious, there seemed something ponderous about her that impressed me deeply, as if she'd quietly cast herself into vast contemplation of this world and everything that lay within it.

Passing through the Barossa wine country high above Adelaide later that afternoon, I began to understand why Anna was striking such a chord with me once again: I was now almost the age she had been when I met her. And perhaps, like she had been then, I was also a bit dazed and disorientated, and very much in search of a home.

Anna, I should explain, was deeply attached to Europe and wanted to stay. In contrast to the open spaces and freshness that so attracted me to Australia, she loved the culture and 'oldness' of Europe. In the only petulant outburst I remember her making, she once said the idea of returning to Adelaide killed her – 'It's so *dull*, no one ever does anything there!' Oddly enough this was also very much how I felt about Ireland before I'd left for Australia.

Although her Jewish father had been forced to escape Germany around the time of the war, Anna had no success in getting a passport from the German authorities. But she was unsettled and, as I now came to appreciate, perhaps overwhelmed from all her experiences since leaving home.

Calling over to her flat one day we found her in tears. In an uncharacteristic rage, she explained that her Italian landlady had just ripped her off on her deposit. She was powerless and the landlady knew it; as an illegal, she could hardly call the police. This finally snapped her resistance and shortly after she reluctantly left Italy to return home to Australia.

Descending in darkness from the high plateau down to Adelaide that evening, I thought about my imminent return to Ireland and almost felt like grieving. It was as if a vibrant part of my life were about to end. So I was distinctly curious to see how life had treated Anna on her return and I determined to contact her the next day.

I found her father's number in an old address book, but it was no longer in service when I rang it the following morning. If he had been forced to leave Nazi Germany he could no longer be a young man. Perhaps he had moved; he may even have died. I hung up the receiver and looked pensively out the cracked glass of the phone box.

I had a sudden sense that there really was no point in talking. Whatever was left for me to do before leaving Australia, whatever business I felt remained unfinished, I had to take care of myself. Perhaps the disconnected number was a sign for me to just move on.

And so it was perhaps very timely that the next day I reached the Nullarbor desert and set off on my solo journey across what is the most isolated stretch of road on the Australian continent.

Crossing the Nullarbor

A rain-soaked wind whipped across the highway before me as I drove north the following day along the coastal plain from Adelaide to Port Augusta. After topping up with petrol and a hot meal in Port Augusta, I pulled out of the service station only to be met by a road marker just barely visible through the streaming rain. 'Perth 2500km' it starkly read.

Roadkill, presumably the victims of road-trains, littered the highway for the next few hundred kilometres. Ploughing into a fifteen stone kangaroo hardly scratched them. But knowing it'd be quite a different story with Bertha, I drove on carefully through the heavy rain. That afternoon as the weather cleared and more of the landscape became visible, I became increasingly confused. This was meant to be the 'null-arbor', the 'no-tree' desert, but trees covered the countryside as far as the eye could see.

The winter light was giving out so, deciding to leave aside this semantic inconsistency until the morning, I pulled in just past the hamlet of Ceduna (meaning, appropriately, in Aborigine, 'a place to sit down and rest'). Nothing could compare to the cold of Bathurst; but that night the wind beat unmercifully against the car panelling and as I folded down the back seats and lay out my mattress, I felt like an Antarctic explorer in his cramped tent sheltering against the savage elements outside.

I was to enjoy my journey across the desert. For those few days I had all the space and solitude I could care for to daydream or chatter out loud to myself as I drove, hour after hour. Stopping each afternoon at dusk, by the dim car-light

I'd chop up some parsnips, potatoes and carrots and drop them into the bubbling pot. (I'd stocked up with a large supply of fruit and vegetables in Adelaide's Asian Market which, together with a few salt crackers and tinned soup, was to feed me crossing the Nullarbor.) When the vegetables were done, I'd garnish them in the dark with salt and pepper (and probably the odd insect) and eat it all piping hot before settling down to sleep.

That evening in Ceduna, as my food cooked, I switched off the light – a dead car battery in such an isolated spot would have spelt serious trouble – and put a cassette reading of Byron's Don Juan into the stereo. Accompanied only by the stove's hissing blue flame, I listened to the words and laughed out loud at Byron's scathing satire on human affairs. He may have been writing about the foibles and pretensions of a society two centuries before in faraway Europe, but nestled in that station wagon on a roadside hundreds of kilometres from civilisation, I thought, how little things ever really change.

A pale, pre-dawn light suffused the inside of the car and woke me early the next morning. Ten hours of driving lay ahead and I was soon on my way. For the next few hours the tree colour changed from glossy-green to gum-tree, smoky brown. Then, just as I passed a stone road marker thirty kilometres before the Nullarbor Roadhouse service station, the tree cover abruptly disappeared. Now I understood what the Nullarbor truly was – nothing but foot-high scrub and spinifex stretched out before me, all the way to the low, milky curve of the horizon.

Unlike Rob, who had seen many emus when he travelled this road two years before, I saw none in those few days. However, there was plenty of other wildlife to distract me on my long drive. Birds of prey, mostly hawks, hovered high in the sky for minutes at a time, eying out their scurrying prey in the desert below before suddenly swooping. Then, from the invisibility of the scrub, they would rise up, beating their wings heavily as a live snake or small animal wriggled helplessly in their talons.

But perhaps the wedge-tail eagles were the most impressive creatures I spotted along my journey. Perfectly camouflaged by their beautiful grey and brown plumage against the dusty desert landscape, and with their massively powerful bodies and wing span of up to ten feet, they were the largest flying birds I was to see in Australia. The desert was their domain and they seemed to treat intruders with disdain. As scavengers, they fed well on the abundant roadkill along the highway and hurtling towards them at a hundred kilometres an hour, by reverse logic, it was they who seemed to intimidate me. Perched atop another picked-clean carcass, only at the last instant would they lethargically beat their wings and sneeringly fly away from me and the approaching vehicle.

On my left, just after passing the Nullarbor Roadhouse, I caught my first glimpses of the ocean. This was the Great Australian Bight, the large scooped-out underbelly of the continental coastline. Soon, spotting the unusual presence of a side-road off the highway, I bumped along its unsealed surface down to the ocean cliffside. A road-train driver, his feet up on the dashboard, was munching sandwiches and looking out over the waves meditatively. I walked down to the cliff edge to stretch my legs and turning my gaze east and west saw nothing but high, rugged cliffs cascading precipitously down into the sparkling Southern Ocean.

I was now nearing the Western Australia border and the spot where John Eyre lost Baxter, his sole white travelling companion, while crossing this interminable desert in the 1840s. As he was out tending the horses, two of the Aborigine trackers killed Baxter. On hearing the commotion, Eyre returned quickly to the camp.

Years later Eyre was to vividly describe his feelings on seeing the body of his dead companion.

'For an instant, I was almost tempted to wish that it had been my fate instead of his. The horrors of the situation glared upon me in such startling reality as for an instant almost to paralyse the mind. At the dead hour of night, in the wildest and most inhospitable wastes of Australia . . . I was left with a single native, whose fidelity I could not rely upon. . . . Three days had passed since we left the last water. . . . Six hundred miles of country had to be traversed before I could hope to obtain the slightest aid or assistance of any kind, whilst I knew not that a single drop of water or an ounce of flour had been left by these murderers from a stock that had previously been so small.'

Although he recovered some supplies, he was still in a horrible position. The two other Aborigines continued to shadow their route a short distance behind trying to entice the remaining Aborigine, Wylie, to join them. Still unsure about Wylie's loyalty after several days alone in the desert, Eyre accepted that he had no choice but to place his faith in him; alone, he couldn't possibly survive the ordeal ahead. The other Aborigines soon gave up hope of stealing the rest of the supplies or of Wylie joining them, and drifted away.

Over the next two winter months, desperately short of water and food, Eyre and Wylie continued their arduous crossing of the Nullarbor. Like Shackleton, Crean and Worsley staggering into the almost inaccessible whaling station on South Georgia Island eighty years later, when finally in July they reached the town of Albany on the south west coast, the astonished inhabitants who encountered them were profoundly moved. Their journey had been considered so very near impossible and Eyre had long since been given up for dead. So the locals looked on in awe as both figures appeared on their streets like two phantoms emerging out of the Hades of the Australian bush.

The Western Australian border – which I crossed that afternoon – is the result of a strange footnote in history. In the fifteenth century, to settle a dispute between two great powers, the Pope proclaimed the Tordesillas Line as the demarcation of the western hemisphere's areas of influence between the Spanish and Portuguese. The 'anti-meridian' on the other side of the globe came to roughly divide Australia along what is now the Western Australian border. Partly as a consequence, I was now in a different time zone and three quarters of an hour ahead of Southern Australia. Later the next day I was to leap forward another forty five minutes just past Caiguna.

As a ghostly light seeped into the shell of the car the next morning near Cocklebiddy, I was still in my sleeping-bag. Sleepily, I rolled down the fogged-up window to let in some cold air and saw a band of pink light lying along the eastern horizon. I was soon up and attending to my normal morning routine. Lifting the bonnet, I checked the oil and radiator; then I removed the spare oil-tank and the water container from the car roof, where I kept them at night away from animals, and stowed them back in the car; then, in the bitter predawn cold, I got going.

My hands were now freezing and, sliding each one in turn under my thigh to warm them up, I kept an eye out for the few remaining kangaroos still out night-feeding. Shifting hands yet again, I glanced from habit in the rear-view mirror – there was little point in doing so, as there was never any traffic on the road this early.

But something did appear in my rear and side view mirrors that morning. A glittering sun was now creeping up slowly over the drowsy horizon behind me. Each time I looked in my mirrors it completely blinded me. It was as if a gigantic, silently moving road-train were bearing down upon me, dazzling me with its powerful headlights. For almost an hour the sun stayed in my mirrors, and watching it reanimate the lifeless desert I came to understand the gasping, almost fearful awe it had inspired in ancient people and why they idolised it as the bringer of all life and power. The rising sun gradually melted the night-frost and turned the desert into a thick sea of rising gray vapour. It had now become a shimmering heath from which I half expected a demented King Lear to appear at any moment. It was truly spectral.

Excluding brief stops at isolated servos, I talked with no one for those four days driving across the Nullarbor, but I never for a moment felt lonely. Hour after hour I'd babble out loud inside the empty car to friends and family whom I hadn't seen for so long and each night, lying down to sleep, I'd feel warmed and nourished by a sense of connection with those physically so far away.

That afternoon, two thousand kilometres after leaving Port Augusta, I reached the small town of Norseman on the edge of the Western Australia goldfields. After the chill of the desert, the air was finally warm and in celebration I bought an ice cream, obviously a minor luxury judging by the fact that it was the first I had seen on sale for several days.

Norseman was not named after a nineteenth-century Scandinavian swagman as I'd expected. Rather, it was the name of a horse that once stumbled over what seemed to be a large rock. His rider, on closer inspection, discovered a large gold nugget and by so doing ignited a gold rush in another part of what proved to be one of Australia's richest gold mining territories.

And arriving soon afterwards into the amalgamated towns of Kalgoorlie/Coolgardie, the centre of Western Australia's goldfields, I learned more about those heady days. A statue to Paddy Hannon, the Irishman who first found gold here in 1893, stands prominently in the town. His discovery, and the gold rush that followed, saved the colony of Western Australia, which, after fifty years struggling to survive in this dry land, was then on its last legs. Only the massive influx of gold money, and settlers seeking it, ensured the colony's eventual survival and prosperity.

The big challenge in extracting the gold was not labour – swagmen down on their luck were more than prepared to trek the five hundred kilometres from the coast for lucrative work – the problem was water. Perth had plenty of water reserves, but the settlement was more than five hundred kilometres away along a mostly uphill course. To pipe it to the goldfields to sustain the workers was considered an impossible task, until an Irish engineer named C. Y. O'Connor took it on. A heavy drinker, and under severe pressure, he gave way to despair and killed himself in 1902, the year before his pipeline finally reached one of the richest seams of gold in the world.

Kalgoorlie, in contrast to some of the other mining towns I'd seen in Australia, has a distinctly American Wild West feel to it. Hannon Street seemed wide enough to turn a covered wagon in and is home to several tall, ornate, western-style saloons. Dropping into the York Hotel bar, I half expected to see can-can girls and tobacco-chewing, whiskey-drinking cowboys leaning against a sawdust bar counter. But this *was* Australia and, instead, I encountered a mob of brawny, red-faced men in thongs, shorts and vests drinking beer at the bar.

It was two o'clock in the afternoon and after a week of solid driving I only wanted a decent cup of coffee. But hearing the sharp banter and the salacious remarks being exchanged between the men and the two female customers, I ordered a manly beer. But the place was rough and I didn't stay long.

After a final night in the bush just past Kalgoorlie, I drove the last five hundred kilometres through drizzling rain to Perth. Rob had arranged with his sister, Jacqui, to put me up for a few nights. I was to meet Rory the next day at the airport; my solitary travels were almost at an end.

Driving alone across the continent had brought me to a wonderful place – a deep womb of healing solitude – and I was loath to leave it. But the sight of Perth's rain-sparkling skyscrapers appearing like a mirage through the miry downpour soon pulled me back to earth. I was now at the Indian Ocean and in the most isolated state capital in the world – Adelaide was over 2,700 kilometres behind me. After seeing only bush for so long, this beautiful, crisp, clean city struck me as something from a futurist science fiction film. Utterly isolated on the edge of the most isolated continent in the globe, it simply had no right to be here.

But there'd be plenty of time for admiration the next day. For now, the first thing I had to do was find Jacqui and get myself a bed for the night.

Perth

In typical Australian style, Jacqui arranged for me to stay in a friend's house. That evening a few people called over and a party ensued. Still in the house the next morning, all five revellers decided to accompany me to the airport to greet Rory. Seeing me surrounded by my newfound friends Rory asked in surprise had I been in Perth long. 'Nay, just got here last night,' I told him. 'Seems a friendly place though.'

After my long drive I wanted to take it easy for a while, so for the next few days we just pottered around Perth. We also visited Fremantle, less than half an hour from the city. Sitting at the mouth of the Swan River, it was here that Captain Fremantle landed in 1829 with the first settlers to establish the colony of Western Australia.

'Freo' has been beautifully restored and retains a very strong nineteenth-century feel, reinforced by the presence of the imposing prison built by transported convicts. The building remained in use as a jail until severe riots in 1988 – during which a slaughter was only just averted when the general inmates nearly broke into the sexual offenders' segregated area – led to it being shut down. It is now open as an historical site to visitors.

Our guide, a retired prison warder, knew the prison well and gave some graphic descriptions of the conditions and events that had taken place inside during his time in service. He also showed us the gallows and the birch, both of which were used as recently as the 1960s. The birch itself had taken over from the cat o' nine tails which, surprisingly, was still used on prisoners as late as 1943.

Overhearing Rory and me chatting, the guide broke into a wide smile. 'Well seems we have some Irish visitors today, folks! Either of you ever hear of a bloke named John Boyle O'Reilly?' Seeing our blank faces, he continued. 'He was quite a fella. He was one of the Fenian leaders and he was transported down here on the last convict ship to Australia in 1868. Anyway, he managed to escape to Boston where he was feted by the Irish-Americans. But obviously some good Aussie ways had rubbed off on him as he proved not to be someone to forget his mates.

'So in 1876 he chartered a US vessel, the *Catalpa*, and sailed back across the ocean.' He pointed past the prison chapel to the sea. 'He moored just a few miles offshore out there, in international waters. He managed to get six of his fellow Fenians out of the prison and across in a rowing boat to the waiting ship, with the guards firing on them. But Boyle O'Reilly was a clever fella. Once they were on board and out into international waters just out there past Rockingham, Boyle gave the order to run up the Stars and Stripes and the soldiers had to stop firing.' The guide chuckled, greatly amused. 'Otherwise, you see, they'd be shooting on "America". The *Catalpa* got clean away and Boyle O'Reilly returned to Boston an even greater hero than before!'

A few days later we set out into the ocean ourselves, to Rottenest Island. Usually a pleasant two-hour jaunt from Perth, the day was very windy and as the ferry swung out of the Swan estuary into the ocean, it was clear we were in for a rough crossing. Almost immediately, the crew fastened down the doors and hatches and, lurching from seat to seat, handed out sick bags to the passengers whose faces were quickly changing from day-tripper smiles to vapid green. Despite the bags, some passengers failed to find their target and in no time the cabin floor was awash with diced brown food particles, swishing back and forth with the violent rocking of the boat.

Luckily Rory and myself were among the very few not to vomit and on docking, we watched the misfortunate crew pass through the boat with large bin-liners to collect the snugly packed paper-bags most people had been clutching carefully for the previous half hour.

One woman, however, kept a hand over her mouth and her full sick bag firmly in her grasp. When Rory gestured that she might like to dump it with a crew member, she just gave a tiny shake of her head and scurried off to the toilet. When she returned she still look green and very embarrassed.

'I'm sorry if I seemed a bit rude back there, but you see when I threw up my dentures came out too and I've just had to fish them out in the toilets. I'm very touchy about my dentures. I've been married twenty-three years and my husband's never seen me without them. So I was hardly going to let a boatload of strangers see me gummy, now was I?'

Rottenest was named by William de Vlamingh, a seventeenth-century Dutch explorer. Landing on the island and spotting the tiny rodent-like animals hopping about the countryside, he named the place Rotteneste, or Rats' Nest, which over time elided into Rottenest. Despite their long tails, the animals, named Quokkas and which are only found on Rottenest, aren't rodents but marsupials. And we didn't have long to wait to spot several of these miniature kangaroos bounding about the road as tamely as squirrels as we walked to the island's campsite.

Although I'd known Rory for years and he was a good friend, we'd never travelled together and our different backpacking styles soon became apparent. My attitude to travel, evinced by my rather slapdash approach to car maintenance, was more casual than Rory's. I wasn't too fussed about travel conditions so long as I kept moving. Rory, on the other hand – although generally laidback and amusing – found some of the 'back-to-nature' aspects of outback travelling a little distasteful. I tended towards the Oscar in our odd couple, and he towards the Felix. But we quickly sorted out any niggles while in Rottenest and our Western Australian journey was to be a great success.

Returning to Perth after three days, we set our minds on preparations for a journey up the west coast to Darwin. As much for the company as for the petrol money, we decided to take on two more passengers. After quickly discounting three young Irish girls, we met the second respondents to our car-share notices, Monika and Detlef, one evening in a pub in Perth's Northbridge area.

Monika, we saw immediately, had a great warmness about her. Sticking out her hand, she introduced herself in a thick Bavarian accent to which Rory, always one to make an impression, replied in clipped, stage German. 'Hello, my name is Ro-ree. Dat is gut, ya?!' Rather than take offence, Monika broke out into a loud belly-laugh and Rory and I quickly exchanged glances. She was in.

In comparison, Detlef seemed a cooler customer. Although travelling separately, like Monika he was a German in his early thirties. With his slim athletic figure, glinting blue eyes and wavy fair hair, he looked like a German officer just stepped out of a 1960s war movie. But as Rory stepped up the banter, it was obvious that Detlef had a wickedly dry sense of humour and was more than a match for him. We gelled. The conversation flowed. The atmosphere was right. And after a few drinks we parted for the evening with arrangements in place to leave the following day.

Western Australia

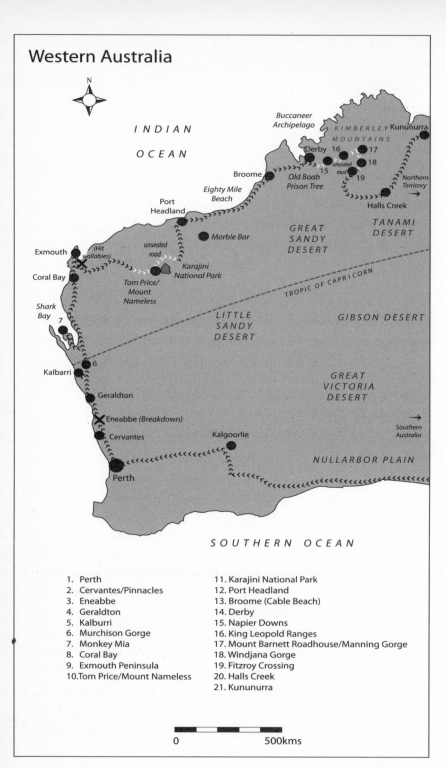

Western Australia

N

INDIAN OCEAN

Buccaneer Archipelago
KIMBERLEY MOUNTAINS
Kununurra
Derby 16   17
                18
15 unsealed road 19
Broome   Northern
Old Boab   Territory →
Prison Tree
Eighty Mile   Halls Creek
Beach

Port
Headland
GREAT   TANAMI
SANDY   DESERT
DESERT

Marble Bar

Exmouth   (Hit   unsealed
          wallabies) road

Coral Bay   Tom Price/   Karajini
            Mount   National Park
            Nameless   TROPIC OF CAPRICORN

Shark
Bay   7
              LITTLE   GIBSON DESERT
              SANDY
              DESERT

Kalbarri   6
                          GREAT
Geraldton   VICTORIA
                          DESERT

Eneabbe (Breakdown)
                                    →
Cervantes   Southern
                                    Australia
            Kalgoorlie

Perth   NULLARBOR PLAIN

SOUTHERN OCEAN

1. Perth
2. Cervantes/Pinnacles
3. Eneabbe
4. Geraldton
5. Kalburri
6. Murchison Gorge
7. Monkey Mia
8. Coral Bay
9. Exmouth Peninsula
10. Tom Price/Mount Nameless

11. Karajini National Park
12. Port Headland
13. Broome (Cable Beach)
14. Derby
15. Napier Downs
16. King Leopold Ranges
17. Mount Barnett Roadhouse/Manning Gorge
18. Windjana Gorge
19. Fitzroy Crossing
20. Halls Creek
21. Kununurra

0   500kms

The Pinnacles to Carnarvon

The plight of an Irish mother can be a terrible thing and from my occasional calls back home I could sense that I was becoming an ever-growing source of despair. Nothing was said, but the undertone was clear. Just *what* was I doing? Would I not now think about settling down and getting a real job?

Given this touching maternal concern, I was delighted to learn that it was partly nagging from his mother that had finally brought Rory to Australia. A wonderfully independent woman, widowed early, his mother had travelled alone to Australia several years before. Now seeing Rory stuck in a job he obviously loathed – a common experience among young graduates in the mid-nineties – she'd encouraged him to get the hell out of the country, go travelling and return to Ireland a bigger person. So, to escape her repeated encouragements, he left.

But a month after his arrival, when Rory rang to say he was leaving the decent job he'd just picked up in Sydney to go travelling with me to Western Australia, motherly exasperation crept into her voice for the first time.

'Western Australia?! But why, Rory? There's *nothing* there!'

Her remark came into my mind as we left Perth the next day as, perhaps for the first time since leaving Sydney, I asked myself, 'My God, what if she's right?' What if for the four thousand kilometres between here and Darwin there really *was* nothing but a few beaches, the odd service station and an awful lot of kangaroos? There were then only about 1.5 million people in Western Australia, eighty percent of them living around Perth. So if three hundred thousand people were scattered around an area larger than Western Europe, there could hardly be a soul to be found in the rest of the state. My only research to date was to learn that Broome was about three quarters the way up the coast; I'd once seen a documentary on the Kimberleys in the very north-western tip of the continent; but, besides that, well. . . .

But luckily we had two Germans on board. Even before we left greater Perth, they began proposing an itinerary for our journey. And from what they said there did indeed seem places worth seeing in this vast state. First up, they suggested, the Pinnacles, about two hours north of Perth.

Another benefit of travelling with Germans was that, unlike most English-speaking backpackers in Australia, they didn't blindly follow the instructions of either the *Lonely Planet* or *Rough Guide* travel books. Their information was refreshingly different from the pool of historical facts, recommendations and urban myths I'd heard repeated *ad nauseam* in so many backpacker pubs and hostels throughout Australia.

So when Monika offered to roughly translate for us what her German guidebook had to say about the Pinnacles, Rory and I gladly accepted. 'The Pinnacles,' Monika began hesitantly, deferring occasionally to Detlef for a more complicated word – being an engineer, his English was excellent – 'are large sandstone columns stretching from one to five metres high. They cover an area of about six square kilometres and their strange appearance convinced the first Dutch explorers, when they saw them from the sea, that they were in fact the ruins of an ancient civilisation. Scientists, however, say they were formed by sand gathering around the base of uprooted trees which over the centuries gradually turned them to stone.'

Strolling peacefully around these preternatural rock formations just before sunset, gazing up at their almost perfect, column-like forms, it was easy to understand the early Dutch explorers' confusion. And as the sun slowly set we stared around as if we were among the ruins of a civilization lost to the world like Atlantis or Easter Island. For the first time in an age, utter silence caressed our eardrums, broken only by the occasional melodic twitter of unseen birds.

Reeling from the silence and this sudden leap into the natural world, we walked calmly back to the car. Detlef was the only one to comment, and his precise German pronouncement seemed to sum it up perfectly. 'That,' he declared, 'is a *very* special place'.

The next morning in a playful mood we set off north again, and just before Eneabbe we had the first of what were to be our journey's eleven punctures. In an uncanny repetition of events after my blowout the year before in Northern New South Wales, we removed our bags to extract the spare. Only then did we find that it was as flat as a pancake. The others looked dismayed. But I broke into nervous laughter. A flat spare tyre didn't strike them as something to laugh about, but they hadn't just travelled four thousand kilometres alone across the continent with a dud spare. We were now only thirty kilometres away from the nearest servo and a car passed every ten minutes. But on the Nullarbor I was often two hundred kilometres from the nearest garage and travelling on a ghost road. I had just had a very lucky escape.

Feeling great relief, I volunteered to look after things and, dragging the spare to the roadside, I hitched a lift with the first passing vehicle, which happened to be a police car. The wheel in the boot, we set off and only then did I notice that it was driven by a very attractive female officer. The dashboard and space between the handbrake and the seats were stuffed with empty coffee cups and iced-coffee cartons. Catching my amused look – by driving for excessive hours with the help of caffeine boosts we both knew she was breaking the law – she blushed and looked even sexier than before.

As drivers covering vast distances tend to speed, drive for long hours or fall asleep at the wheel, at that time Australia had very high road fatalities. Brutally honest road safety campaigns were created to tackle it years before their kind arrived in Ireland. Billboards, displaying mangled cars and bandaged bodies, littered the highway, with blunt slogans like 'Drive, Revive, Survive.'

Not exactly following the official line, the policewoman chuckled like a mischievous schoolgirl and held up the iced coffee she'd been drinking. 'Been driving since seven this morning. This stuff, loud music and AC [air conditioning] are the only things keeping me going.'

She was on her way from Carnarvon to Perth, a journey of almost a thousand kilometres, on what she told me was 'urgent police business'. But her obvious excitement and the fetching cocktail dress lying across the back seat made me suspect that a different type of engagement had called her away so urgently.

Forty minutes later, the tyre repaired and the wheel replaced, we were back on the road.

That night in the Belair Caravan park in Geraldton (an odd name, I thought, for somewhere located just besides a heavily polluted industrial wharf) Monika announced it was her birthday. This was the perfect excuse to inaugurate what was to become a ritual as we purchased, and polished off, a ten-dollar, four-litre, cask of wine. Heady from the wine, the newfound friendship and the sense of freedom, we spent a happy evening together under the stars discussing our journey and much more besides.

Repairing another puncture the following morning, I met a Cork woman who had been in Australia since the 1970s. She loved the country and asked was I going to stay – as if the problem of a obtaining a resident's visa couldn't possibly exist. She looked around her, towards the ocean and up at the sunny sky, and said, 'sure, why would you ever want to leave this place? What more could you ever wish for?' And at that very moment, I couldn't think of a single reason.

The crew of the *Batavia*, a Dutch ship which broke up off the nearby coast in 1660, however might have more readily provided one. After being marooned on the Houtman Abrolhos islands just off the coast, the captain, Francisco Pelsaert, set sail with some of his senior officers and passengers on the ship's pinnacle for modern-day Jakarta in the Dutch East Indies, leaving behind 256 men, women and children on the waterless islands.

On his return two months later he found that a *Lord of the Flies* scenario had taken place among the shipwreck survivors. Soon splitting into two camps after Pelsaert had left to find help, murder, mutilation and rape had become so rampant that only 131 people remained alive when the captain returned. The commander immediately arrested the mutineers and sentenced them to flogging, keelhauling, being dropped from the yard arm or simple execution. Two of the mutineers, however, being younger and perhaps considered less culpable, were condemned to what was viewed as a lighter punishment: they were marooned about three hundred kilometres up the coast near modern-day Shark Bay.

Besides accommodating these two young mutineers, Shark Bay also has the distinction of being the site of the first recorded European landing in Australia in 1616. To mark the landing spot, Dirk Hartog nailed an inscribed metal plate to a post along the beach, which, extraordinarily, William De Vlamingh found still in place seventy years later. The plate now rests in an Amsterdam museum.

Shark Bay still seemed a cut-off place when we reached nearby Kalbarri the next day. Enquiring in the local shop, I learnt that even the Saturday newspapers didn't arrive until Monday. Not even seven hundred kilometres from Perth, we seemed to have already entered the vast oblivion that is Western Australia.

As we whiled away the worst heat of the day at Red Bluff, swimming or reading in the shade, Kalbarri on that August afternoon seemed far, far away from the world. In a daze I wrote a letter to a sister I hadn't seen in over two years and felt as if she were a character from a book I'd once read. Ireland, my family and friends seemed like only vague wisps of a world I could now hardly recall.

In the slight cool of the late afternoon, we drove twenty kilometres of unsealed road up to Murchison Gorge. Opening the car doors we encountered our first swarms of blowflies and knew we were now in the outback proper. The sun had a bite to it too, and lathering on factor thirty sunscreen, we climbed up to the ridge of the gorge to look down at the stratified rock dropping down in a sheer wall to the river and valley-floor below.

Later, as we ambled along the flower-dappled, grassy bank of the river singing *Heidi* for Monika's amusement, two stately emus stepped out fifty metres in front of us. Their fluff of feathers looked like hands linked behind their backs and, with their erect gait, they had the bearing of two tall, meditative, middle-aged men strolling along a riverside path on a Sunday afternoon discussing the more pressing matters of the world. It was uncanny how human they appeared and how utterly indifferent they were to us as they continued along their way in this landscape of towering red stone.

It was the dolphins which had brought us to Shark Bay; or, more specifically, the Blue Nose variety which since the 1960s have been coming daily to this stretch of beach in Monkey Mia. This was one of the few locations in Western Australia where I remember seeing tour buses. The four dolphins which appeared that day had their every movement snapped or recorded by the aging tourists with their standard-issue camcorders. It seemed like a long way to come to visit Sea World and we left after breakfast.

Another puncture and wheel change later, we arrived hot and tired in

Carnarvon and went our separate ways to take care of domestic needs. Rory and Detlef went to 'Woolies' (Woolworths) for food shopping, Monika did some laundry and I took Bertha off to a servo; the roads were taking their toll and Bertha now needed three new tyres. It had been a rotten day and that evening we sat out by the barbie, sizzling steaks and fish, and knocked back the four-litre cask of wine the lads had had the foresight to purchase.

As our good spirits returned, we discussed 'where to next'. Mount Augustus, twice the size of Uluru, and the world's largest rock, was 450 kilometres directly inland but mostly on unsealed roads not suited to a conventional car. So that was quickly scotched.

Detlef then casually mentioned a place on the Exmouth Peninsula with good reef diving called Coral Bay, which a girl in Perth had told him about. It seemed as good idea as any.

The Exmouth Peninsula

Crossing the Tropic of Capricorn just south of the Exmouth Peninsula, we soon arrived at Coral Bay and the Ningaloo Reef.

In contrast to the many young European backpackers to be found in Cairns and along the Great Barrier Reef on the east coast, the few tourists we met in Coral Bay were almost exclusively Australian retirees. Mostly in their late fifties and sixties, several told us that they'd sold up their houses in the main suburbs and were now travelling – some for years at a time – around their native land in luxurious mobile homes, seeing its wonderful sights often for the first time in their lives.

And it was during this tranquil time in Coral Bay that I came to grasp the reason why we made such good travelling companions: we had the right balance. We enjoyed our own company equally as well as each other's, meaning that none of us ever felt crowded. Arriving anywhere new we'd automatically take to our individual pursuits: reading, writing up our diaries or letters, doing laundry or just wandering off for a swim or a long solitary walk.

And it was along Coral Bay beach one afternoon that I met Detlef looking equally as dreamy as me, walking in the opposite direction. 'There are sharks up there,' he said, passing by me without another word of explanation. A few minutes later I spotted a middle-aged man twenty metres out in the ocean looking intently down into the water. 'Ever seen a shark up-close?' he asked, lifting up his head. 'Come in and have a look?'

I was by now so long immersed in Australia's wonders, that I waded in thinking it the most natural thing in the world to do. And soon I was standing in waist-high water as a dozen sinister shapes, each about a metre long, skulked around me in the sea.

'Reef sharks, mate. Beauts, aren't they?' the man said as a metre-wide manta ray glided past like a giant underwater bat. 'It's the Great Whites ya gotta look out for. These little beauties wouldn't touch ya,' he said, standing spellbound gazing at the sharks. 'You look about as big to them as they are to you. You're safe enough with Reefies.' And for the next twenty minutes we stood silently watching these creatures weave all around, so near to us that if I'd reached in I could have touched them. Taking my leave, I thanked the man and waded slowly back to shore.

After a few days of swimming and snorkelling over the waving, iridescent plants and the exotic fish of the reef, we crossed to the ocean side of the Peninsula to visit the Cape Range National Park. We were now well off Highway 1, the road which threads its way along much of the Western Australian coast from Perth to Darwin, and were entering the most isolated area we would encounter before the Kimberleys.

It was due to its remote location that this area was chosen as a military zone decades before and, rounding the tip of the peninsula, we spotted the highest of the joint US/Australian naval base's thirteen communication towers soaring incongruously four hundred metres into the outback sky.

This base, like many others in Australia, indirectly has its origins in the attack on Pearl Harbour. The Japanese strike on the US fleet in December 1941 came, albeit in a less clamorous way, almost as much of a shock to Australia as it did to Americans. Suddenly, Australians were fully aware that their vast coastline – the longest of any country in the world – was hugely vulnerable not only to Japanese raids, but to full-scale invasion.

However, Churchill, with other things on his mind, failed to appreciate these real concerns and pressurised the former colony not to recall any of its Middle Eastern troops to defend their homeland. But John Curtin, the wartime Labor prime minister – who, poignantly like Roosevelt, was to die, partly from exhaustion, only weeks before the end of the war – ignored Churchill's calls and brought many of the troops home.

And three weeks later, in an otherwise obscure article on page four of the

Melbourne Herald, he signalled a seismic and lasting shift in Australia's foreign policy that this move represented.

'We know the problems that the United Kingdom faces,' he wrote. 'We know the constant threat of invasion. We know the dangers of dispersal of strength, but we know, too, that Australia can go and Britain can still hold on ... Without any inhibitions of any kind, I make it quite clear that Australia looks to America, free of any pangs as to our traditional links or kinship with the United Kingdom.'

Curtin, very hard-headedly, had foreseen that Australia needed a new protector; mother England would no longer serve. And in doing so, he forged an alliance with the United States that would protect Australia, but would also continue to draw its forces into America's wars for decades to come.

Shortly after this policy change, one of the first US military bases on Australian soil was built here on the Exmouth Peninsula. Originally built as an advance submarine refuelling base, it was later destroyed in a cyclone in 1945. However, in 1967 the current joint US/Australian military telecommunications base was constructed on the peninsula and was to play an important strategic role during the Cold War.

But these political intrigues were far from our minds as we pitched camp along the seaside scrub that evening. In the absence of facilities, the next day I had an early morning wash in the ocean and was met by a stern-faced Rory watching me disapprovingly as I came out of the water.

'Bet you didn't see that getting in, did you?' he asked pointing down to the cloudy water. Dozens of stingrays had been sunning themselves in sandy shallows and when we threw a stone in they quickly scattered away into deeper water. After this encounter, Rory insisted that we check with the ranger to know if we were likely to encounter any more biting, stinging or snarling creatures while on the peninsula.

'Sharks, mate?! Nah! I wouldn't worry about them. The salties [saltwater crocodiles] have got 'em all by now!' came the ranger's glib response to our enquiry.

'Nay, seriously, guys,' he waited to see how well his practised joke had gone down – I'd heard the very same line from a ranger in a Cape Tribulation – 'there are no salties around here. They don't come this far south. But you ought to keep an eye out for the sharks. We've haven't lost anyone to them yet, at least not round this region, but they do swim in these waters so be careful.

'Ah yeah, there are two things you should also look out for,' he added as we were turning to leave. 'Don't run into the water cos there's plenty of sting rays all around here and if you frighten them they'll whip up their tails and can give you a nasty injury with their barb. Had a French fella in here last year, had to dress up a wound right here,' he said pointing to the very top of his inner thigh. 'Almost lost his crown jewels, just millimetres off. He was some lucky bastard.'

Seeing how much he was enjoying himself, I began to wonder if he had many visitors. 'Two things you said,' Detlef reminded him. 'What was the other?'

'Ah yeah, snakes. Some are venomous around here. But the sea snakes are the real buggers. Real curious bastards sometimes. Might see you swimming and come over for a dekko. You look to them like a strange blob in the water but just ignore 'em. They usually get bored and just swim away. But they're pretty poisonous so you don't wanna go annoying them. So don't move suddenly. They might take fright and bite ya.' He looked up at us again. 'But besides that you should have a great time on the peninsula, beaut place, really is. Ireland and Germany you say?' he confirmed. 'Righto.' And taking up a biro he jotted our details into his visitors' book, giving us our signal to leave.

That afternoon we visited the first of the many spectacular gorges we were to see over the next few weeks in Western Australia.

Skipping along like a mountain goat, Detlef led us over the rocks of Yardie Creek Gorge. Near dusk, just as the darkening light turned the gorge a subtle, silvery gray, the first black-footed wallabies began to emerge. Charmed by the sight, we stayed longer than we ought to and when we finally set off dozens of wallabies had already come out along the roadside. Driving slowly along the unsealed road back to the campsite, we gazed in delight as the wallabies sat on their haunches, twitched their noses or nibbled grass in their tiny front paws while looking up at Bertha's large, curiously white, growling shape making her way through their habitat.

With darkness descending rapidly, the marsupials began to hurtle across our path. And as hundreds had now appeared, the inevitable soon occurred. One shot out from the roadside and smacked at full speed against Bertha's front bumper. Quickly hopping out with our torches, we found the creature lying motionless ten metres back along the road.

Apprehensive about animal bites and tetanus shots, the men stood back. But Monika had no such inhibitions and, immediately going down on her hunkers, she lifted the wallaby up onto her lap, cradling it like a baby.

As the driver, I felt particularly horrified. We had intruded. We didn't belong. And now this animal lay dying before us. His hind legs were clearly broken. And then he started coughing dryly. Monika continued to cradle him, oblivious to the dangers of infections or the blood now trickling from the side of his mouth.

What could we do? We were in almost pitch darkness; heavy cloud cover blocked out what little moonlight there may have been. Exmouth, the nearest habitation, was over a hundred kilometres, or an hour and a half's drive, away. And we would be almost certain to hit more wallabies on the way. Even then, arriving after eight in the evening, would we be able to find a vet's clinic open? And what if the wallaby were to suddenly revive in the car and, alarmed, start kicking wildly to escape?

We all looked down silently on the tiny bundle Monika was petting and soothing on her lap. There seemed only one thing we could do. Finally I spoke up.

'Seems we'll have to put him out of his misery.' The others looked at me as if the thought had only just come to them. But how to do it? Grim suggestions were offered. Rory said we could break his neck. Detlef suggested we suffocate him. 'There is a simpler way,' I piped up. 'Smash a rock on his head.' For a moment no one moved. Then, without a word, Detlef picked up a fist-sized rock and gently pushed Rory aside. Then nodding to Monika to move back, he brought the rock down with a hollow thud on the wallaby's head. The animal immediately went limp and Detlef threw the rock away in disgust.

After the elation of the afternoon, the trek around the spectacular gorge echoing with birdsong, and the endless stream of marsupials along the roadside, we were now dejected. We still had almost thirty kilometres to travel and with four sets of eyes glued to the road and to the bush on both sides, we proceeded at a snail's pace.

We soon hit another wallaby and on hearing the thud and seeing the animal go down, we all groaned. But mercifully he scrambled up again and sat back on his haunches, clearly stunned. The shock soon wore off and he hobbled away like a struck-dog, leaving us to continue back to the tents.

For light and cheer, we lit a fire back at our camp and cooked dinner over the stove. Slowly, animated by the flames and our sense of togetherness underneath the cloud-covered stars, our usual fun and chatter began again. In the inky darkness, not even the flickering flame of the campfire could find the familiar faces and we only knew the others were near by the sound of our voices.

We were in bed by nine in readiness for a dawn rising, but at about midnight the skies split open, sending wind and rain crashing down on our canvas roofs. In danger of being washed away, we quickly pulled up the tents, tossed them, ourselves and everything else into the car, and drove towards the ranger's station a short distance off.

As the torrents pounded down on the tin veranda roof above us, we made tea on the stove and, climbing into our sleeping bags, we chatted and joked for hours until, lulled by the rain, we finally fell fast asleep.

The Pilbara

By the hissing of the stove on that rainy night, we discussed our next destination. Whenever we were at a loss about where to go next, Detlef always called upon the suggestions made to him by a girl he had met in his Perth hostel. To date her advice had proven infallible and once again she came good.

'She recommended an amazing place, a national park, just inland from here in the Pilbara. Karinini or Karajini. Something like that.' At night it sounded like a good idea but reading up on it in daylight we were less sure. The Pilbara, the guidebook said, is one of the hottest places on earth. During the summer of 1923-24 the town of Marble Arch had the longest hot spell in recorded meteorological history when, for 160 days and nights, the temperature never fell below 37.8 Celsius (100 Fahrenheit). Once the temperature was even 49C, over 120 degrees!

But the plan had been made so we backtracked two hundred kilometres to reach Highway 1. Then proceeding north for another two hours, we headed inland towards the town of Tom Price, the nearest point to Karijini.

Except for short detours to the Pinnacles and Kalbarri, we'd stuck to Highway 1, and sealed roads, ever since leaving Perth. But in torrential rain we hit a dirt road seventy kilometres short of town and, negotiating our way through the quagmire, we better appreciated the necessity of a four-wheel-drive vehicle in the outback.

Finally reaching town, our troubles weren't over as the campsite was now a bog. Another midnight wash-out was too much to contemplate so throwing expense to the wind, we checked into a motel.

Most hostels in Australia at that time cost from ten to fifteen dollars a night. But since leaving Perth, except for the occasional seven dollar a night campsite, we had slept in the bush for free. However, the Pilbara is a rich iron-ore and gas mining area, so we shouldn't have been too surprised that the cheapest accommodation in town cost fifty-five dollars a night. For this we got a poky, dirty room furnished with two sagging single beds, an armchair and Gideon's bible.

Rory immediately surveyed the room with a touch of repugnance and bringing our attention to the small, dark deposits on the threadbare carpet, insisted they were rodent droppings. We were all aware that Monika as the only female would be sleeping in one of the two beds. The question now was, who would get the other?

A night on the floor, Rory insisted, and you'd wake up perforated by rat bites. But after showering, Detlef and I emerged so tired, relaxed and utterly indifferent to the perilous conditions that Rory got the bed. It may have been a cunning stratagem on Rory's part, but in either case both Detlef and I, happily enough, woke up unblemished the following morning.

The rain cleared overnight and a glorious, sun-washed day greeted us at breakfast. Far from the oppressive heat we'd expected, Tom Price was comparatively cool. This was unsurprising as at seven hundred metres above sea level, Tom Price is the highest town in Western Australia and even in summer it only gets up to a maximum 35 degrees Celcius. Checking into the dried-out campsite that afternoon, we spread our mattresses and towels out to dry as we lay in the sun reading, writing our diaries, sleeping and generally enjoying our restful day.

Towards late afternoon, we set off to climb Mount Nameless, which at a modest 1130 metres is the highest accessible mountain in the state. The climb was hot but well worth it, as from the summit we looked down on the brown, almost cardboard cut-out, buildings of the mines and iron-ore freighting service in the valley below.

Tired after our trek, back in the campsite we read on the grass before preparing dinner. An Australian retiree came over to use the barbeque and amused us while his dinner cooked. Tom Price, he explained, was an American geologist who came over in the 1950s to survey the area and discovered it had rich minerals. 'But coming down from the hills in the heat one day, the old ticker gave in and he croaked of a heart attack. Least they could do was name the place after him.'

When his steak was almost done, he let rip with a string of Irish jokes. We responded with Australian equivalents. It was all good fun. But then he came out with an odd one-liner. 'Hey, ya hear Lady Di was killed in a car crash?' We waited for the punchline. But with a sudden seriousness, he insisted he wasn't kidding. 'It's all over the news. Come 'round to my mobile and watch the news if yer still don't believe me. The ABC news comes on at seven.'

Still doubtful, we arrived just before the hour. Even if he was only having us on, at least we could enjoy the luxury of an air-conditioned mobile home, a television and maybe a cold beer. He handed us beers and introduced his wife, an attractive woman in her late forties, as she cleaned up after dinner. With beers in our hands, he switched on the telly and we watched as the ABC (Australian Broadcasting Corporation) logo flashed on the screen and the headlines appeared.

So he hadn't been kidding.

News reports came in from all over the world and were relayed to this tiny television set, deep in the outback, two thousand kilometres from the nearest city. Only when the solemn, silver-haired English news-reader announced her death did I really believe it. This was the first BBC news report I'd seen in over two years and its authority was indisputable.

Leaving the town of Tom Price the following morning, we soon arrived at Karijini National Park.

I'd heard countless stories from backpackers in Sydney about the wondrous places to visit on the continent and by now I'd seen most of them: Cradle Mountain in Tasmania, Byron Bay, Fraser Island, the Whitsundays, the Great Barrier Reef, King's Canyon, Uluru, the Great Ocean Road, the Nullarbor and the Pinnacles. But in those two years in Sydney I never once heard the name of Karijini; which is strange, because I thought it the most stunning place I saw in Australia.

Karijini National Park is composed of a series of gorges and waterfalls and we spent three days in rapture wandering about Circular Pool, Weano Gorge,

Oxers Lookout, Hancock Gorge and Fortesque Falls, marvelling at this national park which was like something out of *Indiana Jones*.

In the cul-de-sac canyon of Dale Gorge we stepped along the resplendent, natural tile floor – each block as symmetrical as anything on Northern Ireland's Giant's Causeway – knowing that the rock floor wouldn't have looked out of place in any five star hotel lobby.

Handrail gorge went beyond fantasy. Wading in the shallow river, we pursued its course as it wound through a narrow passageway in the mountain. Then the secret tunnel gave out to the sky as the passageway broke through into the cliff wall of a much larger gorge. A safe distance from the precipice, we then held firmly to the tunnel walls and peered down as the water cascaded into the deeper river gorge below.

A children's story writer could hardly have conjured it up. It was enchanting!

Ghosts of the Past

Driving hour after hour in the outback, we rarely conversed; it was usually too hot and – especially on unsealed roads – often too noisy. So we read, slept, or just gazed out the ochre-tinged windows at the passing landscape. Even as the driver, you could generally switch off as, except for kangaroos near twilight, there were few road hazards and little oncoming traffic. Indeed, I became so casual and dreamy a driver that by now I generally drove barefoot with one foot akimbo on the seat, the other alternating between the automatic's dual pedals of accelerator and brake.

I remember well my daydreaming leaving Karajini that day. Because after all we'd experienced on our travels, from this time onwards I felt that I was now in a world only a child could imagine; one of wonder, colour and endless time. Driving through the Nullarbor Desert, I was coming to realise, had had an effect on me like passing through a long tunnel, and exiting it in Western Australia I emerged into clear, bright sunshine. It was as if a gust of wind had shot right though me, flushing out all my mental cobwebs, and leaving me with an unquenchable thirst for everything that lay all around me.

I didn't look for an intellectual explanation for this; it was just a state of being. But perhaps Yeats's poem 'Those Images' might have come nearest:

> What if I bade you leave
> The cavern of the mind?
> There's better exercise
> In the sunlight and wind.

And the word that kept echoing inside my mind throughout the rest of this trip was *magnificence*. I felt saturated by a sense of the *magnificence* of things and perhaps for the first time in my life I felt as if I were standing face-to-face with the sumptuousness of the natural world.

Towards dusk, as we watched a sun like a glittering blood orange dip slowly behind the horizon, the first outlying houses of Broome began to appear along the roadside. After travelling for over six hours that day in sweltering heat, we were looking forward to stopping for a few days in this celebrated town. But then, with just minutes to go, the car cut out and I knew immediately that we'd run out of petrol.

I hitched to town and an hour later an NRMA mechanic, sporting the local fashion of a shaggy ZZ Top beard reaching down to his navel, picked me up by the phone box from where I'd called him. We drove back to Bertha mostly in silence so as not to wake his young son lying asleep between us in the truck cab. But when I finally made out Bertha's long, pale outline in the darkness I was puzzled to see that four figures were standing alongside her. Pulling in, I was introduced to Scotty, a small, neatly bearded man in his sixties who'd stopped when he saw the breakdown.

Driving back to town with the mechanic to fill up the spare fuel can, I remarked on Scotty's odd accent and asked where he came from. Already taking me for an imbecile for running out of petrol, he gave me a withering look. 'Scotty's from Scotland,' he explained dryly.

After twenty minutes of cold silence, I was relieved when he finally dropped me back at the car with the full fuel can. Soon back on the road, Rory told me that Scotty had stowed away to Australia from his native Glasgow as a fifteen-year-old. That was forty years ago, and he had never been back since. 'He stayed chatting to us because he liked the sound of my accent. Made him think of home, he said.'

Approaching town, I had to brake sharply to avoid a drunken, middle-aged Aboriginal woman staggering in the middle of the pitch-dark road. Had we not been going very slowly and keeping a keen eye out for kangaroos, we would almost certainly have knocked her down.

It had been an eventful day, and I was glad when I finally switched off the engine outside the hostel in Broome.

Walking along the talcum-powder sand of Cable Beach the following morning, it wasn't hard to see why, along with Whitehaven Beach in the Whitsundays, it is often considered the finest beach on the whole continent. Its name derives from the fact that the first telegraph cable across the Indian Ocean to Java was laid from here in 1889. From Java, via Singapore, India, Aden, Egypt, Malta and Gibraltar, the telegraph connected Australia with England, the British Empire and the rest of the world.

There we spent the morning swimming and relaxing before going our various ways after lunch. After rattling over the deep crenulations of the Pilbara's dirt roads I now found that all but two of the car's light bulbs were broken. Replacing them in a local garage – as well as repairing our sixth puncture – I then made my way to the town cemetery.

To my surprise, many of the older gravestones only showed the deceased's name (or nickname) and year of death. This anonymity, it seems, was in keeping with Broome's notoriety, which lasted for at least the first few decades after its foundation in the 1860s, for attracting buccaneers. Often with shady pasts, many of these men might not have talked freely about their true identities or their origins. Several Irish nuns who had worked in the mission in the early part of the twentieth century are also buried in the graveyard. But perhaps most intriguing of all were the many Japanese headstones – for which the cemetery is well-known.

We repeatedly encountered Japanese associations during our time in Broome; not only in the cemetery I visited that day, but also in the historical links, as well as an unexpectedly pleasant evening in Broome's Sun Cinema.

Due to pearling, Broome prospered in the late nineteenth century to such an extent that by the First World War the town supplied eighty percent of the world's mother-of-pearl, then the essential material for manufacturing buttons. But it was a dangerous occupation. In the most calamitous accident of the period, 150 sailors were killed in 1908 when a cyclone caught the fleet unawares out at sea.

To take up jobs as divers and fishermen, Japanese people soon began arriving. Settling in Broome, they quickly became an established part of the community. This made the internment order at the outbreak of the Second World War all the more traumatic for the town, as crew-mates and friends were now obliged to round up the five hundred Broome townspeople of Japanese origin – many of whom were actually Australian-born – who came under the order.

Relationships were further complicated by the Japanese bombing of Broome in 1942. It was a particularly tragic event, as many of the victims were Dutch women and children recently evacuated by seaplane from Java. Due to the tides, the seaplanes landed at night more than a kilometre from land. Accordingly, the less mobile passengers, usually the elderly and women with young children, tended to spend the first night on the seaplanes rather than undertake the long trek over the mudflats and along the lengthy jetty in darkness and laden down with luggage.

So when the zeros came in on 3 March and made towards the flying boats moored out at sea, many Dutch civilians were asleep onboard. Some escaped by swimming to shore but many were killed by the attacking planes or burned to death by the fires sparked off in the leaking aircraft fuel. Some, it is thought, were also killed by sharks. It is estimated that seventy people lost their lives in the attack.

As if in keeping with this theme, the film showing in the open-air Sun Cinema that evening was *Paradise Road*. A typical enough 'uplifting story about the power of the human spirit', it centred on a group of Dutch and English women in a Japanese POW camp.

Sitting on an old deck chair, under a canopy of stars in surroundings that had hardly altered since the cinema first opened in 1916, we stared up entranced at the silver screen. And for two hours, as the story unfolded, the previous century seemed to slip away, transporting us back to a time when stoic characters and simpler ways prevailed and when this rugged town was still the pearling capital of the world.

Despite the many visitors, we found few obvious tourist attractions in town. But Broome's tiny museum which we visited on our last day intrigued me mostly on account of one exhibit. A standard canvas school map of Western Australia, dated 1978 (coincidentally the year of Bertha's manufacture) showed that, with its very few roads, Western Australia was then almost inaccessible.

Several roads extended along the coast near Perth; one went eastwards into the Kalgoorlie goldfields; another went north from Perth without even reaching Geraldton, only four hundred kilometres distant.

But what struck me most was that *the Nullarbor highway didn't exist.* This journey that I was now undertaking with reasonable ease would have been almost impossible just twenty years before. It was startling to consider that up to so recently Western Australia had been cut off from the rest of the continent and in many ways really was still pioneer territory.

Boab trees, with their smooth, bottle-shaped trunks and witch-arm branches stretching out to the sky are a spectral but common sight in this part of the outback. But the next day coming into Derby we stopped at one that is quite unique.

Named the 'Old Prison Tree', this hollow, 1500-year-old tree served in the latter half of the nineteenth century as an overnight holding jail for Aborigines being escorted down from the Kimberleys for trial in Broome.

Climbing through the narrow slit entrance of the tree – perhaps no more than a metre by a metre and a half – two of us could stand up comfortably inside the hollow trunk. Blotches of sunshine and currents of air broke through gaps in the leafy roof and, in contrast to the scorching heat outside, it felt wonderfully cool. It certainly made for a very different type of jail cell than any other I'd seen in Australia.

After stocking up with a week's supply of food for our journey into the Kimberleys, late that afternoon I drove down towards the ocean for some time alone, hoping for a refreshing swim. But emerging out from a thick canopy of trees, I was met by the sight not of yet another spectacular Western Australian beach, but by a seashore mired in mangroves. Beside the mangroves a sign warned of the dangers in the area of saltwater crocodiles which put paid to my swim. So I sat down on the jetty instead and stared out to sea.

It was along this King Sound coastline that William Dampier landed in 1688 and became the first Englishman to set foot on Australian soil. The honour could hardly have fallen to a more colourful man. Originally a pirate – he even named one of his discoveries Buccaneer Archipelago – his account of his Australian voyage, published in 1697, so intrigued King William III that he appointed Dampier a naval captain and sent him back to the region on an official voyage of discovery.

Although often recognised as one of the best map-makers in the history of the British navy, Dampier seems to have been a poor leader of men. His main failing, it can be deduced from reports, was his highly violent disposition. Back in England, after one voyage, a court-martial convicted him of excessive cruelty to a subordinate in His Majesty's Royal Navy, an extraordinary finding in such brutal times.

An expedition he led in the South Pacific inadvertently created one of the greatest stories of all time. After a bitter dispute, one of his officers elected to be marooned on a deserted island five thousand kilometres off the Chilean coast rather than remain under his command. Passing by chance through the same waters again several years later, Dampier picked up the castaway. The man was Alexander Selkirk, later fictionalised by Daniel Defoe as Robinson Crusoe.

Given his violent nature, it is perhaps unsurprising that in 1700 Dampier was recorded as the first European to have killed an Aborigine after a skirmish took place while the Englishmen were gathering water. Later, Dampier gave appalling descriptions of the Aborigines and the terrain of Western Australia, which are generally credited as a main reason why no English ship was sent to further explore Australia until Cook's famous *Endeavour* voyage seventy years later.

Watching the buttery sun melt slowly along the plum-coloured horizon that evening I realised that my explorations certainly paled in comparison; but still, I had travelled far. The next day we'd be leaving for the Kimberleys which ever since I'd arrived in Australia had seemed to me the most isolated and mythical place I could visit on the continent. After this it seemed there was nowhere further I could travel. But after two years in the country, as my return to Ireland seemed imminent, was there now anything that had changed in me, or in how I viewed the world? Yanked out of this luscious life, back in the settled life of work, suburbia and familiar faces, how would I feel inside to know that these few years had ever happened?

And as much as I mulled it over that evening staring out to sea, it was a question I couldn't properly answer.

In sharp contrast to the unsullied wonders of this natural paradise, an incident that night dragged me back again to the rough-edged ways of the world to which I would soon return.

Visiting such isolated places, we rarely met other backpackers in Western Australia. But in the campsite that night two other tents were pitched beside ours. The lads were still up drinking when we went to bed and with nothing separating us except a few metres and a sheet of canvas, we could hear every word of their conversation.

After midnight only two accents remained: one English, one Northern Irish. The 1998 Good Friday agreement would be signed six months later and as peace talks were prominent in the news, I soon heard the English voice ask the other what he reckoned would come of them.

'Ah nothin', came the sharp reply. 'The Catholics and us, well we're really not too fussed about each other, ya know. See down South, it's all run by priests. They've no roads or industry or nothin' – just a few farms. And they jump when the priests tell 'em to. That's why we call 'em boggies. They're really only dreaming if they want us to join them. They're all just wasting their time coz that's *never* gonna happen!'

Rolling over on my camp mat, I threw my eyes up to the canvas roof and wondered whether all the talk of the then roaring Celtic Tiger had just been a Vatican plot. Recalling the Israeli girls' reaction to Tay in Cairns the year before, why, I mused, did every irruption from the outside world seem so discordant here in the virgin wilderness of Australia?

Thank God, I thought, that the next morning possibly the greatest outback wilderness awaited us. What joy to be turning our backs on the world, and to be venturing as deeply as I would ever go into the splendid isolation in this most remote of continents.

The Kimberleys

Leaving Derby the next morning I was so lost in a daydream that I completely failed to notice when the bitumen road gave out about sixty kilometres north of town and we all but crash-landed onto the dirt road. The horrific jolt popped the rear-view mirror out of its fitting and as it fell onto the passenger seat Rory, Monika and Detlef all broke into hysterics. Suddenly wide awake, and seeing the humour of it all, I just chucked the mirror on top of our gear in the back of the car. We'd hardly be needing *that* in the Kimberleys.

The main hazard of unsealed roads, besides the occasional flash flood, are the bumpy ruts four-wheel-drive tyres leave on the track. This can frequently make driving a very bone-rattling experience. Fortunately for us a grader – a hybrid bulldozer for smoothing dirt roads – had recently passed over much of the route to Mount Garnett, making the drive a reasonably gentle trip.

In the late afternoon the road brought us through a narrow opening in a high rock wall. Emerging on the other side we saw that four Jackeroos – ranch hands on horse-back – had pulled in and, watched by these silhouetted horse-men, Bertha moved slowly onto the vast, dusty plain of the Napier Downs. The glowing red crests of the distant King Leopold Mountains enclosed the plain, forming a massive natural amphitheatre in the mountainous distance before us.

A half hour later as the light faded, and with just five kilometres to go to our intended campsite, I skidded to a halt. A dip in the road ahead appeared to have turned into a swollen creek and Detlef – ever the engineer – got out to test the water's depth with a stick. Judging it far too deep to cross, we backtracked to a picnic area we'd spotted twenty kilometres earlier. After cooking a simple meal, and exhausted by the heat and dirt-road driving, we soon flaked out in the tents.

Just after dawn we drove out to Lennard Gorge. The track soon became impassable by conventional vehicle and we covered the last six kilometres on foot.

That morning taught me the real meaning of the word 'legion', because that's what the flies were. It was like something from a biblical plague; and after twenty minutes walking through this black pea soup, Rory cracked.

He'd just bought a straw hat in Derby and, swiping around with it, he cursed, lunged and twisted like a dog in high summer trying to swat away the hoards of flies. But it was a futile undertaking; the heat (which for the next few weeks rarely fell below 40 degrees) and the flies were things we just had to deal with. The rest of us walked on, trying as best we could to ignore the insects and to focus on the refreshing swim awaiting us in the gorge.

But the heat and flies must really have been very bad that morning because, for once, even Detlef seemed irritated. A recurring heat allergy, only now he told us, had flared up again and for the last few days his legs and feet – which we now noticed were covered in rashes – had been unbearably itchy.

Reaching the gorge, we dived deep into the cold, sun-glittering pool observed by a sole giant water monitor lying like a miniature dinosaur on a rock-ledge above us. But the swim was all too short, as we had to set off again back to the car before the sun rose too high in the sky.

Back at the campsite, sweat-soaked and exhausted, another trial awaited us. Our camping spot, Marchfly creek, we soon discovered, was very well-named. Marchflies don't just thirstily drink up human sweat like normal, decent flies. No, marchflies are carnivores and they quickly resumed taking lumps out of our flesh, just as they had done the night before. This was simply too much, and despite the suffocating heat, we ate lunch zipped up in our sauna-like tents. But we had to escape these flying piranhas so, breaking with our established practice, immediately after lunch we uprooted the tents and left in the worst heat of the afternoon for Manning Gorge.

It was then that puncture number-eight struck. Changing the wheel, we quickly found that with all the weight of our baggage – we had to keep our rubbish and carry it out of the Kimberleys – the jack simply wouldn't budge. Rory, Detlef and I each in turn had a go, but the car wouldn't move an inch.

But then I had an idea. Digging out a tub of melted margarine, I poured its runny contents along the cogs and joints of the jack. Then, while the three others, neck-veins bulging, lifted up on the back bumper to take some weight off the jack, I pushed with all my strength on the jack handle, and it finally moved. A few minutes later, caked in dust and sweat, we drove on.

When we finally reached Mount Barnett I knew by the fuel price that we were now in the most isolated place in Australia. Near Uluru the year before I'd been amazed to pay over a dollar ($1.01) per litre. Along the Nullarbor I'd paid even higher – $1.05. But at Mount Barnett, just before Manning Gorge, three hundred kilometres into the Kimberleys, it was $1.13. Far from begrudging the cost – supplies after all had to be transported here over huge distances and appalling roads – I looked on it rather as a sign of just how far we'd come from suburban Sydney and its 70-cent per litre fuel prices.

All the troubles of the world we left behind over those next three days in Manning Gorge. Each morning the pre-dawn chorus roused us gently from our sleep. And as the birds burst into their exuberant, melodic song, I'd climb out of the tent, feeling exuberantly alive, to revel in the best part of the outback day.

Grabbing my towel, now dry on the car side mirror, I'd walk the fifty metres to the lake and as the delicate shades of the early morning light became more distinct, I'd swim alone in the crisp, clean pool. Waiting for the others to get up, I'd stretch out with a book and let the warming dawn sunshine dry me.

We spent most of those three days reading, dozing in the nooks of the gorge or swimming in the still, chill water as the birds sang, fluttered and chirped all around us. For the occasional diversion we'd climb up on a rock ledge and jump five metres down into the water below. We ate, drank, talked and read – all the time knowing this was it; we'd finally made it into the Kimberleys, into this secret garden at the world's end.

Knowing we had come as far into the Kimberley as a conventional vehicle would allow, we next headed south-east towards Windjana and Tunnel Creek gorges. Almost inevitably, however, leaving Manning Gorge we had another puncture. The prospect of travelling another three hundred kilometres over unsealed roads to Windjana with only one spare wheel seemed foolhardy; since Derby we had carried two spares for that very reason. So we backtracked thirty-five kilometres to Mount House, an outback station we were told could do repairs.

All the notices I saw in Australia advertising work in outback stations requested girls. Young women were wanted to cook and, more importantly, provide female company for the jackeroos. A South African girl with whom I'd travelled in Fraser Island had spent three months on a station flirting with the jackeroos and feeding them thick steaks for breakfast. She even got engaged to one of them. So I wasn't too surprised to find a Scottish girl from Dumfries minding the small station store. She'd been there for several months, she said, and although the money wasn't great, there was nothing to spend it on and so she had managed to save. It could be boring enough at times, and although she was happy to soon be returning to Sydney, she was glad she had come here. It was an experience, she reckoned, that she'd be able to talk about for the rest of her life.

Due to our puncture, we were still on the road when darkness swooped down and, as we knew only too well from our experience on the Exmouth Peninsula, this was less than ideal. But it wasn't kangaroos that unnerved us. Rather, it was the glowing flames and vast shafts of wood-smoke we spotted ascending in spirals from the hills a few kilometres ahead. It might be a controlled blaze clearing off dangerous scrub and undergrowth, as we'd heard no reports of bushfires. But the glow of the fire and smoke looked very intimidating against the backdrop of the dark outback sky, and an emergency conference was quickly called.

Detlef got right to the point. The straightness of the smoke columns indicated that there was little wind. So if we did drive into a bushfire, Bertha should be able to outpace the flames. With no better proposal offered, his Teutonic logic held sway. Entering the fire area, we were hugely relieved to see that despite the dramatic walls of blazing flames in the scrub on both sides of us, it was indeed a controlled fire.

Overcoming the day's final hazards of close calls with both bounding kangaroos and clusters of roving cattle, we finally arrived into Windjana at 8 PM. It had taken us six hours to travel three hundred kilometres over dirt roads and we were shattered.

After the superlatives of the Pinnacles, the Exmouth Peninsula and Karijini we had almost become a little blasé about visiting another Western Australian natural wonder. But seeing Windjana gorge in sunlight the following morning we were as startled as ever. Would the marvels of Western Australia ever end?

If Karajini was the stuff of Enid Blyton, Windjana must belong to *Peter Pan*, because passing through a slit in the stone wall entrance into the long, high gorge, all we could see were crocodiles. And by their sharp, V-shaped snouts we knew they were Johnsons, or 'Freshies', and in theory harmless. But Rory was adamant that he had seen one with the square snout, a Saltie. Given Rory's track record as a less than hardy traveller, doubts were expressed within the party. But then we noticed at the gorge entrance a sign warning about the dangers of Estuarine (Salties!) crocodiles. Sometimes, it said, they make their way this far inland and caution should be taken; swimming was at one's own risk. It was only then that the unusual presence of a shower block in a national park made ominous sense.

We didn't exercise much caution, however, as we approached within metres to take photographs of the reptiles as they lay on the riverbanks or prowled up and down in the shallow water, their beady eyes and menacing snouts sinisterly surveying the path before them.

After a lengthy early morning trek along the steep path tucked in under the gorge wall, where we luckily evaded the occasional grass snake looped in the branches overhead, we returned to our camp just outside the gorge entrance. After lunching on our standard fare – soup, crackers, tepid tinned pears and a mug of hot tea – the others napped and I sat under a sheltering boab tree to write up my diary. Looking up occasionally from the page, my eyes would meet the grey rock-face rising up vertiginously from the savannah grass. All along its face, clusters of tubular rock formations spiralled and soared heavenwards like gigantic organ pipes. Later, as the light of the descending sun struck the rock, it changed in colour from a steely grey to an ethereal, evanescent pink.

Since entering the Kimberleys, each evening as dinner cooked on the gas stove and the others bustled about in the darkness, I'd lie back on one of the camp mattresses and look up at the stars with Monika's binoculars. Here in the crystal air the night sky was magnificent. Since coming to Australia I'd been convinced that the southern skies were far more spectacular than those in the northern hemisphere. So many more stars seemed visible to the naked eye. And reading Patrick Moore's *The Stars of the Southern Hemisphere* – which had travelled with me all the way from Sydney's Town Hall Library – I noted smugly that he shared my opinion.

And with the book's star charts open beside me, I identified the stars and constellations. There was Orion, the only major constellation visible from both hemispheres. That must be the false Southern Cross (the real Southern Cross wasn't visible this far north, you could only see it in the southern half of

Australia and in New Zealand). There was the Sea of Tranquillity and the other pummelled craters and seas of the moon. Moving my binoculars, I'd be lost in the sights above me until, like a child, I was called for dinner.

On our two-hour drive from Windjana Gorge to Tunnel Creek Gorge, Monika read us the story of Jundumurra.

Jundumurra was an Aborigine who, as a boy, had worked as a tracker for the whites. His astonishing shooting, tracking and horsemanship talents had earned him his English nickname, Pigeon. He was so skilled that many of his own people thought he had magical gifts.

But his life changed in 1894 when he tracked down a group of Aborigines for his white boss, a man named Richardson. They then held them for a week in Lillimilura police station (whose ruins we saw when we were leaving Windjana). Chained together in the police station, the older Aboriginal men talked incessantly to Jundumurra in his own language, asking him why he was helping the whites destroy his own people. Their arguments and persistence finally broke him down and seeing no alternative means to effect their release, he very reluctantly shot Richardson.

Now a wanted man, he took to the life of a guerrilla, attacking white settlers and then slipping back into the bush. His ability to evade capture soon made him legendary, and throughout the continent he became hailed as the Aboriginal Ned Kelly.

For three years after killing Richardson, Jundumurra continued his guerrilla ways, regularly using Tunnel Creek Gorge as a hideout. But by 1897, with most of his men captured, perhaps out of loneliness or despair, he seemed to have lost his fighting spirit and began neglecting his customarily cautious ways.

And later that afternoon, watched by the occasional red-eyed glint of a Johnson crocodile lying on a high rock ledge, we waded by torchlight, often waist-deep, through the 750-metre darkness of Tunnel Creek. Thousands of bats hung from the tunnel roof and we were thankful we were wearing sandals, which protected us from the slime of the bat excrement caking the riverbed. Re-emerging into the sunlight, we reached the tunnel exit where Jundumurra was killed.

In an ironic twist, the man who shot Jundumurra was himself an Aborigine tracker. Standing in that fateful spot, it struck me that in his final moments he must have welcomed leaving this world of such bitter disillusionment.

Corroboree at Fitzroy Crossing

Civilisation, in the form of the Great Northern Highway, greeted us later that day. After more than 500 kilometres of shuddering, unsealed roads, the smooth bitumen surface came like a balm, a true luxury. It was another suffocating day and we looked forward to a cold beer in Fitzroy Crossing. But when we arrived that Sunday afternoon it was like a ghost town. The roads were bleached in white sunlight and the few shops and houses appeared deserted. There was nothing for it but to find our way to the Old Telegraph Office, now a hostel, and check in.

Fitzroy Crossing was one of the original relay points of the telegraph line connecting Darwin with Cable Beach in Broome and, by extension, with the outside world. And on being shown to our airy room – and my first bed since Perth – it was clear that the building had retained much of its original character. With its shaded verandas and even the old telegraph machine still set up in one of the rooms, it evoked the same sense of stepping back in time that we had experienced that special evening in the Sun Cinema in Broome.

To fully appreciate the voluptuous pleasure of a bed and hot shower, one needs to understand that when driving in the outback you are never truly clean. As our only source of air-conditioning was to open the two front windows, ochre dust made its way into *everything*. You could shower and scrub, rinse and wash, but the dust always clung to your skin, hair and clothes. Water never seemed to remove it from your mouth and dust ground into your teeth. Only one drink cut through the dusty taste of the outback – cold beer.

So, checked into the hostel and utterly unconcerned about our filthy appearance, we made our way to the Crossing Inn, the only pub in town. Despite the absence of a map or road sign, it wasn't difficult to find. We only had to follow the piles of crushed beer cans under almost every shady tree. The two stacks nearest the pub were staggering; each must have consisted of at least a thousand cans and both were as high as a Halloween bonfire pile.

As we entered the pub we passed an Aborigine buying a slab (twenty-four bottles) of Emu beer at the bottle shop counter. Though not quite barred, Aborigines aren't particularly welcome in most pubs in this part of Western Australia, partly explaining the small mountains of tin debris visible in most towns in the region.

We'd decided to take a slab back to the hostel ourselves, to imbibe over the course of the afternoon. Only we couldn't decide between Victoria Bitter or the local Emu beer. 'Looks like you'll have to try both,' the barmaid remarked in a lilting Meath accent when we explained our dilemma.

Drinking our first midi – a VB – we asked the barmaid about the sign above the bar: 'No swearing, No spitting, No humbugging'. 'Humbugging?' she answered. 'That just means no talking shite and boring people to death. And trust me, having worked here for a few months, some people really do need the reminder.'

After a second quick round – of Emu this time – we were still no nearer a decision. So we did the only sensible thing and bought a slab of each, and with the two cases tucked under our arms, we made our way back to the hostel.

Taking the hostel's two-man kayak and a generous supply of beer down to the nearby Fitzroy River, we spent the rest of the day in the sun, drinking on empty stomachs and paddling the kayak up and down the river until long after dark.

None of it was very sensible but at least it made for great fun for Monika the following morning as we struggled, near death with hangovers, in the 40-degree heat. I spent the early morning, corpse-like, on the top bunk, lying as near to the thin draft of the ceiling fan as I dared. It helped little. So at about noon I drove into town to loiter in an air-conditioned shop on the pretext of buying a carton of orange juice. I delayed so long near the fridges that I heard the full hourly news bulletin which announced the deaths of Mother Teresa and Don Bradman's wife. Coming so quickly after Princess Diana's accident, and feeling irreverent in my hangover, I reckoned the patron saint of obituary writers was being unduly kind.

To add to the headache, that afternoon, while wading in Geike Gorge, I was stung by a stingray. I had seen the cloudy water and had the evidence of a cut foot. But being so far from the sea, the others put it down to alcoholic hallucinations. Only later did I read that stingrays, peculiarly, 'are also found in Geike Gorge, near Fitzroy Crossing'. The others, however, remained sceptical.

That evening, Monika came to us as we sprawled in the common room and announced that there was a corroboree (an Aboriginal dance gathering) in town. 'Most of the people around here *are* Aborigine and the old lady who takes care of the hostel tells me there aren't too many genuine corroborees anymore. It starts just across the road from the BP station at 5.30.'

Half an hour later when we reached the edge of the solitary highway cutting through town, the place was bustling with about two hundred Aborigines. Three heavily bosomed, middle-aged Aboriginal women were preparing huge skillets of fruit and meat on a large, makeshift table which they were vigilantly trying to safeguard against the occasional nimble pilferer.

We sat down in the thick dust before the 'stage' area. The stream of overcrowded cars – mostly old battered Holden and Ford sedans – and four-wheel-drives constantly arriving would first disgorge their load, circle the arena, and point their headlights inwards to illuminate the area as night fell. Each arrival was greeted with shouts of friendly slander as the place bustled with noise and loud chatter.

At the back of the arena, two strips of sack cloth hung from stakes to form a shoulder-high screen. Above this, the faces of the performers were visible as they peered over at the growing crowd.

Sitting in the thick dust, I felt like the narrator in a round-the-world travel documentary. Imagining the camera fixed on me, I gazed around agog, maybe even with a little apprehension, at the diverse tribal, almost vaudevillian, activities spiralling away all about me.

The two large woodpiles were lit as darkness came down and suddenly dozens of Aboriginal children – many strangely blond-haired – appeared and began to play footie with empty two-litre plastic bottles, or to tussle together in pairs. The winning wrestler would help his friend off the ground. Then, springing up and twirling jubilantly in the air, he'd zip off to find another playmate. Dancing so wildly around the fires, they looked like swarms of fireflies flitting before the light of two enormous candles.

Then the old men – about half a dozen of them – started up. Chanting and mumbling their tribal songs to the beat of their two clacking boomerang-shaped sticks, the music gave out a soothing rhythm like the sound of slow, giant castanets.

And there were dogs everywhere. Dozens of them, straying in and around the assembled mass, were rewarded by the odd scrap of food or kick in the rump. Rory was frantically trying to ward them off, convinced they were crawling with fleas. (And he was right; later back in the hostel I picked two from the tangle of my leg-hairs.) In front of us sat three Aborigine men and within minutes Rory and myself were reaching for Monika's mosquito repellent – not so much to ward off insects, but simply to take the bite off their body odour, which was so rancid it stung our nostrils.

We sat hour after hour, waiting for things to start. The woodpiles grew lower, our backsides got number, the kids slowed down, and the music of the old men eventually stopped. But still nothing happened.

Eventually, after two hours a young Aborigine, flanked by two elders, walked to the centre of the arena and introduced their troupe, which came from Tennant Creek in the Territories. The rest he explained in an aboriginal language appropriate to the audience (of the several hundred in the audience there were probably no more than twenty whites).

We only stayed for the first three dances. The second was an emu dance. A group of male dancers emerged from behind the sack-cloth screen wearing tall, elaborate, spiralling white headgear and performed their traditional, rhythmic stomp-step dance, their necks jerking and the rest of their movements uncannily mimicking the gait of an emu. I'd seen a similar dance the year before in Alice Springs in perfect imitation of the movements of the kangaroo, and both times their verisimilitude was extraordinary.

The last dance was chilling. Five young Aboriginal men stomped into the arena with wooden prisoner yokes lying across their strong shoulders. Their faces, sticking through large nooses, displayed desperate, forced smiles and their eyes shone maniacally. The loud, joyous Aboriginal colours (red, black and yellow like the Rastafarians) of the yokes and the vigorous dancing contrasted chillingly with the obvious implication of an imprisoned, brutalised people being compelled to smile subserviently to the world.

Later in the hostel common room, we watched an old man shuffle in, short of breath, and sit down heavily on the armchair beside me. He appeared to be travelling with his daughter, a thin woman in her sixties. Despite his impressive mop of long white hair – which earlier through the open bathroom door I'd seen him brush over and over again – he was very elderly (I later discovered that he was almost ninety) and seemingly riddled with arthritis. It crossed my mind that his daughter might be taking him on this one last holiday before his time finally came.

But he seemed far from being on his last legs when he turned to talk with me. Exhilarated by the spectacle he'd just seen, his face beamed with delight as he talked animatedly about the dances and the bustle of the night's corroboree.

'Still,' he paused suddenly thoughtful, 'it doesn't compare with the one I saw just after I got here. October 9th, 1925. That's when I arrived in Australia. I was seventeen then, just off a farm outside Southampton, in the south of England.' Looking suddenly anxious, he asked, 'You've heard of Southampton, haven't you?' I had, I said.

'Well, a few months after I got here I saw a corroboree. It was in New South Wales, just south of the Queensland border. I thought it was wonderful. Wonderful! The dancing and singing and the strangeness of it all.' Telling me this, his eyes lit up. 'But you know, even at the time I thought it very odd. Because when they finished no one clapped or showed any sign of appreciation. The crowd was mostly white and after all this wonderful dancing and singing there was just dead silence.' His earlier energy now seemed to drain out of him.

'Shortly after that corroboree I heard that Aborigines from the same area had been arrested and led away in chains. I don't know why.' He shook his head slowly and his expression quickly returned to that of a weary old man. 'In real chains, you know,' he repeated sadly. 'They led them away in real chains'.

A few minutes later his daughter appeared and brought him by the arm to bed.

The Top End:
Completing the Circle

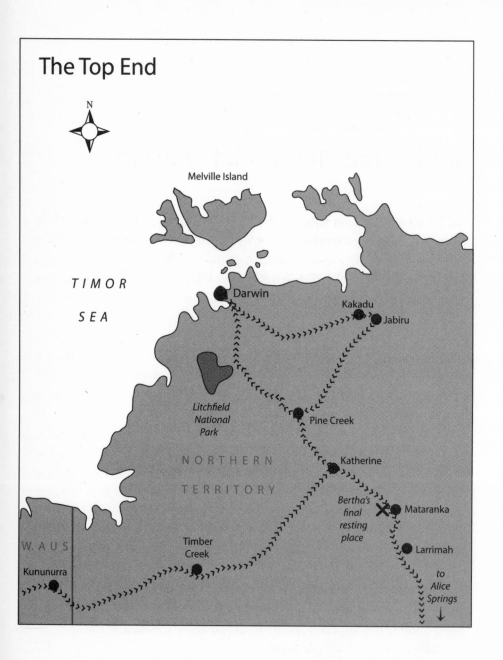

The Top End

N

Melville Island

TIMOR

SEA

Darwin

Kakadu

Jabiru

Litchfield
National
Park

Pine Creek

NORTHERN

TERRITORY

Katherine

Bertha's
final
resting
place

Mataranka

Larrimah

W. AUS

Timber
Creek

to
Alice
Springs

Kununurra

Katherine Gorge and Darwin

Although now back on sealed roads, passing through the small town of Hall's Creek the next day reminded us that we were still in very remote territory. It was from here that two locals had set off several years before on an outback trip, neglecting to tell friends of their destination. This hampered the search when they went missing and it was only two years later that their skeletons were found in the bush alongside their broken-down vehicle.

Kunanurru, our next stop seven hours northwest of Fitzroy Crossing, we read, was an important port and diamond mining region. But we thought it a hell-hole. Crippled by the heat, it was all we could do to put up the tents and make tea before collapsing on camp mats to read by the car-light or just flake out.

We were all exceedingly irritable and everyone bit their tongue. No one felt inclined to cook, and when the usual dinner-time had long passed Rory quietly suggested we get a steak sandwich and a beer from a fast food shop and eat them out in the open. Detlef's heat rash was burning painfully and he didn't want to move, leaving Monika, Rory and me to walk the short distance to town.

A half-hour later, revived by the food, cold beer and slight cool of evening, we sat chatting quietly in the open. But Kunanurru had a palpably edgy feel to it and we felt ill at ease.

Our concerns were justified as shortly afterwards we saw a police car pull up alongside a group of Aborigines about fifty metres away from us. Holding a long baton-torch, an officer got out of the car and approached them.

'Hey guys. Are we alright here?'

'Yes, sir. We are,' came mumbled replies.

'Now you *are* only eating,' he asked, shining the torch from face to face. 'No alcohol? Because if you're drinking, you know, I'll have to put you in the lock-up for the night?' Rory and I discretely hid our beer cans behind our legs but he didn't even look our way. Shining his torch around once more, he slowly got into the squad car and drove off.

For several weeks it had been hard not to notice how alcohol consumption was a weathervane for just how divided this society was. On our first night in Broome we'd walked into a bustling bar only to find we were the only whites in the place. Aborigines stopped talking to stare at us. Feeling as if we had just entered a black bar in 1950s Alabama, we left quickly.

We also learnt in Broome that our usual fare of four-litre casks of wine were not available for purchase in the area. Asking for one from the bottle shop owner, he looked at me uncomfortably and directed me towards the two-litre casks. But I wanted a four-litre cask, I told him. Only then did he tell me that it was illegal to sell four-litre wine casks in this part of the state. He didn't need to explain that anything cheap was drunk by Aborigines. We also discovered that all the local bottle shops closed on welfare cheque day – when Aborigines arrive en masse to collect their money – to prevent them blowing it all on alcohol.

Although there is a serious drink problem among Aborigines – and on our journey we saw plenty of evidence of this – it is all the more striking for being so visible. As Aborigines are rarely welcome in bars, they drink their bottle-shop booze outdoors. As a result they are commonly seen staggering in public places and the debris of their collective drinking is left behind for the whole community to see and judge them by.

Just after the policeman disappeared that night in Kunanurru, a nasty verbal exchange started up between two of the men. Rory raised an eyebrow, but thinking myself well versed in these things, I muttered that we shouldn't worry, shouting is just their way. I was less convinced as the two men started swinging punches at each other up and down the field. Then one was pushed to the ground and the other started kicking him viciously in the stomach and in the head.

'You said you'd have my money!' he screamed as he smashed his boot again into the other's face. 'I want my fuckin' ten dollars back! Do you hear me?!'

'Go easy man, he'll pay up,' came from the group lost in darkness. But no one stepped in. We quickly stood up and left. On the way back to the campsite two separate groups of Aborigines shouted threats at us as we passed. We left town early the following morning.

After almost two months of extraordinary travels, we left Western Australia later that day. Seeing the 'Welcome to the Northern Territories' sign, we changed the car clock back ninety minutes. Now in the Top End, or the northern part of the Northern Territories, we continued on for another five hours to Katherine, the home of perhaps the most famous gorge in Australia.

We were now a trifling three hours' drive from Darwin and, feeling we were almost 'home', we checked into a modern backpacker hostel with hot showers, air-conditioning and a small swimming pool. After roughing it since Perth, we felt we well deserved it.

This was where Detlef left us. On a tighter schedule and feeling he'd seen enough of Outback Australia, he decided to push on by bus to Darwin alone the following morning. From there he'd catch a ferry to Indonesia and continue his travels for another month before returning to Germany. To mark our parting he offered us dinner in the local RSL. Rory and I ate a lump of steak, but not having digested meat for almost two months – it would have been impossible to 'keep' in the heat of the outback without refrigeration – we felt very queasy the next morning.

But that didn't prevent the three of us paddling twenty-four kilometres of the famous gorge (or more correctly thirteen interlocking gorges) over the next two days. As fresh water fills the gorge from wall to wall, it can only be traversed by canoe. Birds' nests overhang the sandstone walls and the water is so perfectly pure we only had to dip our cupped hands overboard to drink. To cool off, we'd simply slip out of our canoes and have a quick swim, knowing that they wouldn't drift far in the still water.

As so few people obtain overnight ranger passes to sleep in the gorge, towards late afternoon we found ourselves virtually alone in the seventh gorge. As we began looking for a place to settle down for the night, a lone canoeist suddenly appeared – from where no one was sure – and attached himself to us. He introduced himself as Sepp and told us in competent English – even though he'd only started speaking the language on his arrival in Australia eight weeks before – that he was a primary school teacher from the southern, Italian-speaking region of Switzerland.

With his scraggily blond beard, elongated face, dishevelled hair and demented eyes he had a striking resemblance to a young Donald Sutherland. And, true to form, considering the pyromaniac character Sutherland played in *Backdraft*, after dragging our canoes up a sand bank, Sepp wasted no time in lighting a fire – even though it was strictly prohibited in the gorge. But after the day's swimming, paddling and carrying of canoes, we were pleased he did and soon we settled down to eat by the flames.

We played cards for a short while after dinner on the soft sand with nothing but a warm starry sky above us. But fatigue soon set in, and putting aside the cards we began to talk quietly, hushed by the peaceful atmosphere of the gorge.

In his broken English, Sepp asked did we like the 'Irish whistle', he'd just taken it up. He was clearly very musical; earlier he had told Rory that his father was the conductor of the Swiss National Orchestra. He usually played the cello, he said, but it wasn't exactly the easiest thing to carry around while backpacking. But he had been practising a tune over the last few weeks which perhaps we might know. And with that, we lay back on our sleeping bags, tired from the day's efforts, and gazed up at the twinkling night sky as the sweet notes of 'Danny Boy' gently echoed down the long sandstone chambers of the deserted gorge. Soothed by the melody – this had to be Arcadia – we soon peacefully drifted off to sleep.

Emotionally, most journeys end before the final destination is reached. And, in many ways, mine ended that night in Katherine Gorge.

More than two years before I had sat on the steps of the Sydney Opera House asking myself why I was here, and in answer could only think of the story of a sailor who after several dark, ice-bound months in the Arctic had returned to see the world through different eyes. And over the last few years I'd travelled through vast distances both in my mind through books, and on land over dusty highways, but I was still only wandering. On Rainbow Beach in Queensland the year before, I had looked up at the massiveness of the silent night sky, and knew that something was missing inside me; that my connection to the natural world, and to the life all around me, was somehow not there, not strong enough. I couldn't sense it breathing. Something in me just wasn't fully alive.

But on that serene night in Katherine Gorge, the last drop fell and in the gentlest of ways something finally broke through.

The sand bank where we were sleeping was in a small side gorge closed in by two high rock walls. Lying down to sleep, I glanced up a final time in awe at the starry, moonless sky. But waking up during the night, I saw that a white, full moon now balanced against the tip of one of the walls above me. Turning over, I fell back to sleep. Waking up later in the night, I saw the glazed, opaque moon now resting against the crest of the gorge's other wall and suddenly I felt enormously comforted. The moon, as it revolved above me, seemed to be sealing off a celestial dome, forming an enormous inverted cradle. And inside this celestial cradle, mother nature seemed to be lulling me lovingly in her protective care.

Even half asleep, I knew my journey was over. The world was no longer inanimate to me. I felt as if I were now completely a part of the natural world. My connection with it had been reopened and it has rarely left me since. Feeling it settling, almost sensuously, inside me, I closed my eyes and felt myself spiralling downwards into a warm, nestling cocoon and within seconds I was sound asleep.

Just before Darwin, we stopped off in Litchfield Park, another national park of water-filled gorges and stunning waterfalls. There we travelled through the rainforest jungle on the worst twenty kilometres of dirt roads and potholes of the whole trip to see the 'Lost City' whose peculiar rock formations convincingly resemble time-eroded Inca temples.

Finally, four thousand kilometres and two months after leaving Perth, we reached Darwin.

Darwin, it's often said, has the most transient population of any Australian town – no one seems to have grown up there but everyone seems to have lived there at some time. But to us it seemed inhabited for the most part by backpackers. This came as a minor culture shock, having met so few since leaving Perth. Uncannily, it also gave me the same sense I had experienced the year before when I arrived into Cairns after travelling up the Queensland coast.

Out the first night, I saw a drunken backpacker walking towards us, a wine glass in one hand and two thick ashtrays in the other; he had to be Irish, no one else would bother to steal bar ashtrays.

'Hey, did you rob them?!' I challenged him in the middle of the street. 'Because if you did, I'll have to report you to the police.' For a moment he looked at me with alarm before quickly breaking into a laugh. The Clonmel man soon became my best buddy, told us the 'ins and outs' of Darwin, gave us his phone number and offered Rory and myself jobs as commercial cleaners to start later that week. Waking up to the sauna heat the next morning, we quickly scotched the notion of working, or of staying more than a few days. And we never saw Clonmel man again.

Given the conditions, most of our days were spent on the large, shaded upstairs balcony, reading or chatting over cold drinks. We were now well used to the 40-degree dry heat of the outback, but in Darwin the temperature was accompanied by crippling humidity. We needed to recuperate, but Darwin was clearly not the place to do it.

Darwin is a new town in every respect. After sighting the harbour in 1839, Captain John Clements Wickham of the HMS *Beagle* named the place in honour of his companion from a previous voyage, Charles Darwin. And for much of the next century and a half, despite a heavy Japanese bombing raid in 1942 in which over four hundred people were killed, the town seemed to enjoy a relatively peaceful existence. That is, until 1974, when Cyclone Tracy all but flattened it.

The meteorological satellite images of the cyclone in the town museum reveal why it was so devastating. One side of the cyclone passed over the town followed by a few minutes of eerie calm as the eye passed over. Then the other side struck and wreaked havoc once more. Most of Darwin's buildings had been made of light materials, so all but the best constructed were destroyed. Following reconstruction, the town is now full of flimsy, rather ugly buildings.

The town prison mostly survived and, wanting to add it to my list, Rory and I paid a visit one burning-hot afternoon.

Arriving outside the open gate, we found the ticket office unattended, and no one inside. So we let ourselves in past the wire fence and wandered alone around the dusty compound baked in white sunshine. We weren't yet in high summer but experiencing the heat of this shadeless jail we could only scratch our sweaty heads in wonderment at how the prisoners – and guards – had withstood it. The medium-security prison even had a corrugated iron roof, which must have turned it into an oven for much of the year.

For most of its existence it seemed to have been a low-security prison, initially for Aborigines and later mainly for petty criminals. A segregation block, however, did exist for prisoners of bad influence or those with contagious diseases, usually leprosy. Later, in the 1970s, this block was used to house Vietnamese boat people attempting to enter the country illegally from the north.

That night we went to the Mindil Beach Market, famous for its many stalls and Asian food, an understandable cultural influence considering that Darwin is less than a thousand kilometres from Indonesia. We had a lovely evening, pottering around and buying food which we then brought down to eat on the beach and watched a red fireball, almost as stunning as the one we'd seen in Broome, dramatically sink beneath the ocean.

After two days of doing little in Darwin except melt, we decided to press on. Kakadu, about two hours south, was our very last stop before heading straight back to Sydney. Rory had the option of flying directly from Darwin to Sydney with one of his internal air tickets, but I persuaded him that by flying he'd miss out on seeing the Central Desert, and also of getting a good feel for the Queensland coast.

In light of subsequent events, his decision not to fly was perhaps unfortunate.

Kakadu and Home

After a late night in one of Darwin's many Irish bars watching the All-Ireland Hurling Final, we set off again the next morning to Kakadu, perhaps the best-known national park in Australia.

We were now back to the pleasures of bush travel, and if not for the dubious luxury of a fly-ridden decompositor toilet, our campsite that night might have been anywhere in the outback. Katherine and Darwin, which are comparatively insect-free, had softened us up and returning to the fly infestation of the bush, we felt like crying. We were shattered and the joys of the outback had worn wafer thin.

Pitching our tents about thirty metres from a billabong (a small oxbow lake) we read the stern warning signs along the riverbank about the dangers of Estuarine Crocodiles and felt uneasy. We didn't need Rory this time to tell us why ours was the only tent in the camping area.

People are terrified of saltwater crocodiles for very good reason. Salties often pick-off water buffalo, cattle, even horses – and sometimes humans – from the water's edge and then, dragging them into deeper water, they twist violently to thrash and eventually drown their prey. Crocodiles, it's not commonly known, can run faster than humans over short distances, so it wasn't hard to see that by camping so near the water we made easy pickings. But we shrugged our shoulders and stayed put, reckoning that if we'd made it this far we'd probably survive this final hazard.

Early the next morning under a heavy, overcast sky, we visited Nourlangie Rock, to where Aborigines traditionally migrate during the stormy season. Weather is critically important to the survival of a nomadic people, and rather than the two seasons (wet and dry) that westerners associate with tropical areas, Aborigines identify six. Each season is associated with a different part of the Kakadu region and a corresponding seasonal activity such as hunting, gathering, hibernating or performing sacred ceremonies.

The migration to Nourlangie Rock (and the onset of the stormy season) was signalled by the appearance of the vivid Alyurr, or Leichhardt dragonfly. Ludwig Leichhardt, after whom the Sydney suburb is named, was a Prussian explorer and in the 1840s was the first white man to visit this area. Describing the Alyurr in his diary of 1847 as 'brick red with blue markings', he disappeared with all his companions on a later expedition. Their traces were never found, although a rumour persisted among Aboriginal tribes in the region that a white man, possibly the last survivor of the expedition, lived with them for decades afterwards.

Knowing the rains were about to break, Aborigines would retreat to the shelter of the over-hangings around Nourlangie rock for protection from the lightning storms that would soon be crashing down around them. During this season they would paint the rock face and perform ceremonies.

And the rock art here leaps out from the mountainside as electrically as the storms which no doubt inspired it. One rock face depicts a Dreaming about lightning, with almost phosphorescent-bright figures etched on the stone.

Lightning, so the Dreamtime goes, was an ancestral spirit who mated with his sister and their offspring was the ginga, the crocodile. The Alyurrs – the vivid Leichhardt dragonflies – are also the offspring of Lightning, and so the Aborigines knew that when they made their annual appearance they were searching for their first father, Lightning, who would soon appear in the form of violent storms.

We had arrived in Kakadu in the driest part of the dry season and the park was cloaked in the subtle but startling light-brown and green hues familiar to us from the outback. But viewing a film of the park through the seasons in the rangers' office, it was clear that in spring, after the winter rains, the place explodes in a riot of colours as lush flora burst forth. Indeed, the wet season downpours are so heavy that the levees usually break around December, creating a vast floodplain.

Being trapped on treetops, many lizards, rodents and smaller marsupials become 'sitting ducks' for the aquatic pythons that slither and swim from oasis to oasis to eat them up. Of course, flooding has no affect on the plentiful Salties in

Kakadu. After being hunted almost to extinction for their skins by the 1960s, when we visited they were back in the area to about 50 percent of their original number of fifty thousand.

Early one evening we went to see more rock art at Ubirr. Arriving near sunset, we watched the sun sparkle off the green wetlands of Arnham land, the Aboriginal territory to the north of Kakadu which are off-limits to whites without an entry permit.

Tagging onto a tour group, we heard the guide point to a drawing high up on a craggy rock face. It was estimated to be four thousand years old and has a remarkable likeness to a Tasmanian Tiger. This indicates, he said, that they probably lived in all parts of Australia in that period. Hearing that, I thought back to my visit to Hobart's rundown museum fifteen months before and the tatty stuffed remains of the last Tasmanian Tiger I'd seen on display there. That was on the continent's southern island state, and here I was now in the Top End. I really had travelled full-circle.

The next morning, worn out but flushed with a quiet sense of triumph, we left Kakadu. Our journey was over. Now all that remained was the incidental matter of a five-thousand-kilometre drive to Sydney and my flight back to Europe.

Our plan was for Monika to travel back with us to Townsville in Queensland. From there she could take a bus north to Cairns for her flight out of the country and Rory and I would continue south down the Queensland and New South Wales coasts to Sydney.

But the best laid plans of mice and men . . . often overlook the importance of a functioning radiator cap.

Leaving Kakadu, I'd seen that ours was a little rusty but, eager to get going and convinced by now that Bertha was all but indestructible, I decided to wait and pick up a new one in Alice Springs. My experience of the blocked plugs and points of the year before, it seemed, had taught me little.

Two hours after leaving Kakadu, just past the small town of Mataranka, we began to smell burning rubber. Probably only the tyres, I thought; it was another sizzling day and no doubt we'd soon be adding another disintegrated tyre to the many strewn by other vehicles along the road. We still had our two spares in the back, so we weren't very concerned. But with each kilometre the smell got stronger. We halted. The tyres seemed fine. We drove on anxiously.

But when the engine began to rattle we knew we were in trouble. Opening the bonnet, billows of smoke gushed out and fearing the worst I glanced down at the radiator. The cap had gone and with nothing to retain the water and steam, the radiator was now bone dry.

I hitched to Larammah and an hour later was picked up by Willie, the NRMA mechanic, and back we drove to Bertha. After a quick look, he decided to tow her in darkness back to Mataranka. I wasn't worried about the cost, the tow would be free – I'd learnt from my experience in Cadney Homestead near Coober Pedy and was now a gold NRMA member. But I had a bad feeling about Bertha this time.

I woke up at dawn in an open field beside Willie's garage. Uneasy about what Willie's verdict would be, I breakfasted alone, lingering over a book for several hours. Bertha had such character, we'd travelled so far together, that now my affection for her was like a cavalryman's for his long-serving, trusty steed. Finally mustering my courage, I walked anxiously into Willie's large work compound.

Willie, it seemed, was a practical outback man and not one given to sugar-coating. Seeing me enter the compound, he glanced across at Bertha and then back at me and pronounced simply, 'Mate, she's fucked!'

What else was there to say? The burning rubber smell of the previous day was caused by the pistons valves melting. I could get a reconditioned engine sent down from Darwin but that'd take a few days and between that and having it installed, the cost would probably be about a thousand dollars – pretty much the value of the car.

'I can give you a hundred bucks for the wheels . . . ' Willie added, pointing to the graveyard of old station wagon wrecks in his large compound, ' . . . but not much use for scrappage round here. That's the best I can do for you, sorry mate.'

Was it only my guilty conscience, or did it feel that it had almost been destined to end like this? Bertha had taken me everywhere in Australia – almost thirty thousand kilometres. And the day we'd left on the very last journey I needed her for – greatly helped by my negligence – she'd given up the ghost. For a moment I felt quite emotional. But somehow it seemed fitting that she'd remain in this elephants' graveyard of twenty- and thirty-year-old station wagons and sedans in the tiny town of Mataranka, Northern Territories.

With a bitter grin, I broke the news to the others who were now having break-fast in the coffee shop. After a few curses, everyone took it in the spirit of the ups

221

and downs of outback travelling. Why we didn't return to Darwin and pick up flights to our two destinations I still don't know. Perhaps by now we were so used to overland travel that catching a bus just seemed the natural thing to do.

In the post office, which doubled as the bus station, we were told that two Greyhound buses passed through each afternoon. One could take Monika, via Three Ways, to Townsville. The other, bound for Sydney, had seats available for Rory and me. Its route, naturally, brought us around the world, via Alice Springs, Adelaide, Canberra and Wagga Wagga. But then what choice did we have?

Rory, of course, whole-heartedly thanked me for dissuading him from flying out of Darwin. Now, he told me in a dry tone, he'd have to fork out three hundred and forty dollars for the pleasure of sitting his arse for fifty-six hours on a bus seat, when instead he could have taken a comfortable four-hour flight from Darwin to Sydney for free – he'd already paid for the internal tickets in Dublin. And as for me . . . being so tight-arsed that I wouldn't even spend three bucks on a new radiator cap, well!

We took whatever we could carry from the car. I brought the tent and gas stove which I reckoned I might be able to sell for a few bucks back in Sydney, and left everything else behind: pots, mattresses, books, cups, plates, cutlery, jumpleads, fuel and water tanks. Early that afternoon, outside the post office/bus stop, we said our goodbyes to Monika, our perfect travelling companion.

An hour later we were aboard a bus heading towards Alice Springs. After the rush of the day's events I relaxed, knowing it was now up to someone else to get me to Sydney. I'd seen a lot of this country in the last two and a half years. I'd seen a lot of all sorts of things. But with my flights from Sydney leaving in under two weeks' time, Ireland and Europe now beckoned.

Over those last few months the constant stream of red outback dust coming in through the car windows had long since found its way into everything onboard. But only then did I notice that it had left a very distinct ochre imprint on the borders of my diary's white pages. Looking up from the pages, I turned towards the bus window and stared out once again over the Simpson desert. The fact that the dust had imprinted itself on the white pages of my diary struck me suddenly as very fitting. Somehow it just felt right.

And looking at that diary as I write this last sentence, it seems that that ochre dust has proven quite indelible – after all these years it's still very much there.

Some Sources

Bruce Chatwin (1988) *Songlines*, Penguin

Manning Clark (1980), *Occasional Writings and Speeches*, Fontana Books, Melbourne

Manning Clark (1981) *A History of Australia I – from the earliest times to the age of Macquarie*, Melbourne University Press.

James Cook (1949), *The Voyages of Captain Cook*, Cresset Press, London

Robyn Davidson (1980) *Tracks*, Pantheon Books, New York

David Davies (1974), *The last of the Tasmanians*, Barnes & Noble Books

E. E. Dunlop, (1986), *The War Diaries of Weary Dunlop – Java and the Burma-Thailand Railway 1942-1945*, Penguin, London

Tim Flannery (1999), *The Explorers – Epic first-hand accounts of exploration in Australia*, Phoenix, London

Lucy Frost, ed. (1992), *The Journal of Annie Baxter Dawbin: July 1858 – May 1868*

Harry Gordon (1976), *An Eyewitness History of Australia*, Rigby, Adelaide, Sydney, Melbourne, Perth, Brisbane

Harry Heseltine, ed. (1972), *The Penguin Book of Australia Verse*, Penguin, Melbourne

Robert Hughes (1987), *The Fatal Shore*, Collins Harvill, London

D. H. Lawrence (1993), *Kangaroo*, Cambridge University Press

Henry Lawson (1966), *The Drover's Wife and Other Stories,* Angus and Robertson, Sydney

David Malouf (1996), *The Conversations at Curlew Creek*, Random House, New York

David Marr (1992), *Patrick White: A Life*, Knopf, New York

Boris Pasternak (1959), *The Last Summer*, Translated by George Reavey, Peter Owen, London

Captain Joshua Slocum (1956), *Sailing Alone Around the World*, Dover, USA

Coultman Smith (1978), *Tales of old Tasmania: The First Fifty Years*, Rigby, Adelaide

Paul Theroux (1995), *The Pillars of Hercules – A Grand Tour of the Mediterranean*, Cape Cod Scriveners Company, USA

Russel Ward (1979), *A Short History of Australia*, Ure Smith

Patrick White (1957), *Voss*, Penguin, Victoria

Patrick White (1976), *A Fringe of Leaves*, Jonathan Cape Ltd, London

Charles Wilson (1988), *Australia, 1788-1988: the Creation of a Nation*, Barnes and Noble, USA